HIGHER EDUCATION
IN TWENTIETH-CENTURY AMERICA

Library of Congress Series in American
Civilization | Edited by Ralph Henry Gabriel

HIGHER EDUCATION

William Clyde DeVane

IN TWENTIETH-CENTURY AMERICA

HARVARD UNIVERSITY PRESS

Cambridge, Massachusetts | 1965

FOREWORD

The visible change in higher education in America since 1900, quickening yearly since the end of World War II, has been so swift that one is likely to underestimate the deeper continuity that persists. Yet that continuity is frequently a more important fact than the change. In this book I have not attempted to write a formal history, but instead I have tried to identify and describe large movements and trends. To illustrate these movements, I have selected certain colleges and universities partly for their excellence in their kind, but even more for their representative quality. In dealing with the rise and development of a movement, moreover, I have sometimes had to risk the charge of repetition as I traced its direction and progress through the several phases of the twentieth century. My aim throughout has been to make use of history to gain an understanding and to make an appraisal of the condition of higher education in America as the present century approaches the two-thirds mark.

In the preparation of this book, I have inevitably incurred many debts, most of which, I hope, I have acknowledged. A few others require separate mention here. I am grateful to Messrs. Holt, Rinehart and Winston, Inc., for permission to quote at some length from Henry Seidel Canby's *Alma Mater*, published in 1936 by their predecessor organization, Farrar and Rinehart. I am also deeply grateful to the editors of *The American Scholar* for allowing me to use "The Dilemma of National Greatness," an article first published in the Autumn 1964 issue of the magazine, as the concluding chapter in the present volume. A by-product of my work on the book, this epilogue permits me to approach the central problem of higher education from a different perspective.

For the year's leave of absence which gave me the leisure to complete the manuscript, as for a great deal else, I am profoundly indebted to Yale University. I must express here, too, my gratitude to three ladies who have generously shared my labors. Mrs. Anne Granger contributed her skill, patience, and warm interest to the preparation of the manuscript. By relieving me of many problems of detail, Miss Katherine Hauschild, my secretary for the last ten years of my tenure as Dean of Yale College, gave me the precious commodity of time. My wife, Mabel Phillips DeVane, gave me her constant wise counsel in the criticism of expression, of ideas, and in the ordering of thought. Her devotion, here as always, has made this book infinitely better than it otherwise might have been.

New Haven, Connecticut   William Clyde DeVane
October 1964

CONTENTS

HIGHER EDUCATION
IN TWENTIETH-CENTURY AMERICA

CHAPTER I | CHARACTERISTICS

It is characteristic of the country that supports our heterogeneous educational establishment, so diverse in size, structure, purpose, and quality, that no strong national organization has ever been created to regulate or standardize it, or even to advise it with authority. Contrary to the European practice, our government has never had a minister of education. The United States Office of Education, a branch of the Department of Health, Education and Welfare, is under the supervision of a commissioner and until very recently has hardly been an administrative agency at all. Its duties have been informative and advisory, and its main concern has been with public secondary education. The reasons for this are mainly historical. First, in the eighteenth and most of the nineteenth century, higher education in America was in the hands of the private colleges and universities, and they had no desire to be controlled by a central authority. Next, the Bureau of Education, as it was called in the beginning, came into existence in the nineteenth century concurrently with the great westward expansion of the country, the strong upsurge of democratic feeling, and the recognition that universal education was necessary for the progress and welfare of the country, indeed for the success of democracy itself. In the East, academies and Latin schools existed to train students for the colleges; in the developing West, the public high schools were established by the communities. The public schools, and later the Land Grant colleges, offered the most promising field for the attention of the new federal bureau.

In spite of the recommendations of several early presidents of the country, Washington and Jefferson among them, no national university was ever established, and to this day the city of Washington is not the educational center that some of our other large cities are. Control of higher education has been left to local private or state initiative. In this climate of laissez faire, there has been a "wild, uncontrolled, and uncritical expansion," shocking to the European but truly in the American grain. In the development of higher education, one may see such national traits as hopefulness, initiative, energy, and practicality finding extravagant expression. In a less attractive vein, we may also see a habitual wastefulness, extremely uneven standards, improvisation, an emphasis upon the immediate and the material, faith in mere bigness and numbers, and a deep-seated anti-intellectualism which is profoundly contradictory to a naive trust that education will somehow magically cure all the country's ills. In both its good and bad aspects, the American educational establishment is a reflection of our democratic society.

The most obvious fact about higher education in the United States in the twentieth century is its swift and enormous increase in size. Each new report confronts us with astonishing figures. In 1900 there were 237,592 resident students in our colleges; in 1950 there were 2,659,021.[1] In 1964 the figure has risen to 4,800,000, and a much larger number is predicted for 1975. These statistics are more than reflections of the country's growth in population. In 1900, 4 percent of the young people between the ages of eighteen and twenty-one were in college; in 1950 the percentage in colleges was estimated to have risen to 20 percent; and in 1964 the figure has risen to almost 35 percent. To care for this vast increase in student enrollment, the country now has more than 2,400 institutions offering education and training beyond the twelfth grade. Less than ten years ago there were 897 colleges of liberal arts, 267 professional and technical schools, 98 teachers' colleges, 510 junior colleges, 83 colleges offering only programs of general education, and a number of others that do not fit into any of these categories.[2] Within each category, with the exception of teachers' colleges, many of which have nominally converted themselves into four-year colleges of liberal arts, there has been a further increase in the number of institutions.

The growth in numbers of students and the institutions caring for them has been overmatched by the value of the physical property these institutions now own. At the beginning of the century, such property was appraised at $254 million. In 1950 the figure had risen to $5.25 billion,[3] and it is now estimated to be more than $8 billion. However much the value of the dollar may have declined, this huge increase in the provision of physical property is characteristic of both the materialistic temper and the generosity of the public. The tremendous increase in the national wealth is also reflected in the greater endowment of higher education. In 1900 the total endowments of our educational institutions amounted to approximately $200 million, a figure smaller than the individual endowment of several of our universities in 1964. In 1950 the total endowment of all universities was about $2.7 billion; today the sum may be more than $5 billion. Because of contracts from the federal government, grants from foundations and industry, and increased tuition charges, the annual income of the universities and colleges has increased even more spectacularly than their endowments.

The diversity of our institutions of higher education, natural enough in the circumstances, is as characteristic as their number. The more than 2,400 universities and colleges of the country vary in point of size from the small independent or church-related colleges of 200 students to the gigantic collection of organizations, colleges, graduate and professional schools, and institutes accommodating 50,000 or more inhabitants, which Clark Kerr calls the multiversity.[4] The typical institution of higher education in the United States is no longer the private college of the late nineteenth century, but rather the state university of moderate size, with a large undergraduate college, a substantial graduate school, and professional schools in medicine, law, and education. Moreover, it is also true that the majority of students in the United States are now attending public rather than private institutions of higher education. But in between the small country college and the multiversity, as large as a city, there are institutions of all conceivable kinds, functions, and quality. Some are liberal residential colleges reminiscent of an earlier day; some are large urban colleges or universities vocationally inclined; some are privately supported, some publicly; some are vast educational complexes; some are primarily teaching institutions, and some are deeply committed to research. Some are quite obscure in spite of their huge size, and others, perhaps a dozen, are now reckoned to be among the great universities of the world. Taken as a whole, these institutions in their variety reflect the history of the nation as it has passed through a time of drastic economic, political, and social change—from an agricultural and frontier society, cut off from international influences, to a culture based on industry, controlled by scientific and technological ideas and forces, and acutely conscious of its place among the nations.

Yet in the face of the variety of our many institutions, we must emphasize the fact that through the whole development of higher education in the United States there runs the increasing purpose to democratize education—the determination to provide free education for all those willing and able to take it. This ideal, so uniquely American, partly idealistic and libertarian and partly practical, moves forward as inevitably as a glacier, but in this century with increasing speed. Today, more than 90 percent of the youth of the country eligible in age are in secondary schools. Most intelligent and liberal citizens of the nineteenth century thought that this stage was as far as the state or community was obligated to carry them. Now the ideal is being projected into higher education as the right of all youth, rather than the privilege of the wealthy. The idea, though not often explicitly stated, was inherent in the founding of state colleges and universities and the Land Grant institutions; it was at work in the establishment of colleges for women; it is active today in the increasing provision of community and junior colleges.

Further, the democratic ideal has brought about the enormous increase in scholarships and fellowships provided by the colleges and universities themselves, by philanthropic foundations and industry, and by the state and national government. It is present in the low tuition charges of public institutions and is an element in recent anti-discrimination and antisegregation movements. In late years it has been increasingly viewed as more than an obligation of society to provide higher education for all who are able to profit by it; it is now seen as a necessary action for the government to take in its own interest. The G.I. Bill for the education of veterans after the Second World War was the payment of a debt that the country owed its defenders. Congressional action in the National Defense Education Act of 1958, as well as in more recent legislation, goes beyond the payment of a debt, to the idea of preparation for the defense, welfare, and health of the society in the future. The whole conception of universal education at the higher level shows American democracy setting itself further in opposition to the old European ideal of higher education only for an elite; and of course the growing financial aids to education ensure that it is not confined to the wealthy, but reaches nearly all groups in our society.

In yet another characteristic aspect, higher education in the United States has differed, in degree at least, from its parent European systems. This is in its fundamental instinct towards practical service. Frederick J. Turner, the historian of the American frontier, in 1893 commented on this trait in these words: "Nothing in our educational history is more striking than the steady pressure of democracy upon its universities to adapt themselves to the requirements of all the people."[5] And this continues to be true. Higher education seems to have tried to meet every demand. This tendency, seen in the number and variety of institutions in the country, is perhaps even better seen in the vast numbers of courses and the extremely heterogeneous subjects of instruction offered by even the most conservative universities, to say nothing of the wares of the more venturesome or pliant institutions.

Internally, higher education in this century has been characterized by a struggle between two conflicting forces—the yearning for stability and the stronger necessity for change. The desire for stability is best seen in the undergraduate college, which dominated the country's educational system at the beginning of the century. In the last hundred years the great fact behind all developments in our world, and consequently in higher education, has been the scientific revolution. American education, always responsive to the pressures of the time, in this era of rapid change reflects more faithfully than ever before in its history the major concerns of the society. Educational patterns tend to harden when they are undisturbed by the pressures of change; thus the old classical curriculum, a legacy from a more stable time, changed only gradually as knowledge, or *scientia,* grew. When, however, the accumulated discoveries in the nineteenth century culminated in a new phase of the scientific revolution, there was something like an explosion of knowledge, and the fixed curriculum of liberal studies was unable to cope with it. The elective system, the first major attempt at a solution, had earlier extended the democratic principle to the studies of the college; the humanities that were the mainstay of the classical curriculum were no more favored than those newer studies, the sciences and the social sciences. But the elective system, which opened the way for the development of the university, left the college in a highly disordered state, and beginning with the second decade of this century the continuing problem in undergraduate education has been to reconstruct a curriculum that would preserve the values of the old studies while including the virtues and content of the new. The struggles towards an ordered arrangement were numerous: subjects were arranged in groups, with the student required to take work in each group; then a curriculum was set up consisting of a program of distribution and a program of concentration; new methods of instruction were adopted; honors work and comprehensive examinations were introduced; and a strong movement in general education flourished.

As will be seen in later chapters of this book, the devices have been insufficient to restore real cohesiveness to the college curriculum, and the fragmentation has not been healed. Yet there is certainly a vitality evidenced in the successive attempts to achieve it. The student and the college at their best are both more serious about the intellectual work to be done, its purpose and its value. Since the Second World War, and especially since the sputniks, the student has become much more highly motivated and is much readier to work up to his potentialities. He frequently enters college with credits towards his degree from advanced-credit examinations, and he is often in a position to take his degree in three years if he so desires. In college he has specialized to an extent unknown by his grandfather, or even his father. He learns a great deal about his field and knows that the country needs and rewards specialists and that he should go on for further training in an advanced school. For three quarters of the graduates of the best colleges in the East, the bachelor's degree has ceased to be a terminal one. The good student is tempted to anticipate the specialization of the graduate school and to embark upon its methods early. The broad liberal studies, which, though not so obviously useful, are most valuable in the maturing process, are inevitably the ones to be squeezed out. This tendency further complicates the problem of attaining cohesiveness in the college curriculum. But even as these struggles were going on, American college education has been improving steadily in quality since 1910, and both the college and its students have drawn up appreciably upon their English and European counterparts.

Another movement, having little direct effect upon academic excellence so far, has caused the colleges, especially of the East, to look back to their origins in Oxford and Cambridge and put a renewed emphasis upon life outside the classroom by encouraging student activities and by building dormitories, student unions, residential quadrangles, "colleges," or "houses." True to their origin, the colleges have recently made a strong attempt to resume the obligation to educate the whole student, socially and morally as well as intellectually.

More characteristic of the twentieth century, however, is the rise to maturity of the American university, an institution that was essentially Germanic in its origin. In its ideal form the university was the conservator and disseminator of knowledge, the encourager of inquiry, speculation, and discovery, and the guardian of the intellect. The heart of the university, as Abraham Flexner said in his *Universities: American, English, German* (1930), was the graduate school of arts and sciences, the professional schools of medicine and law, and a number of institutes for special research. The university was the home of the specialist, particularly of the specialist in the sciences. To the graduate schools, with their natural commitment to specialization rather than breadth, the explosion of knowledge was no problem, and enormous impetus was given to study in the separate fields through departmentalization and intensive research. Far beyond the conservation and dissemination of knowledge, the first obligation here became the advancement of learning—an obligation that gave purpose and direction to the university and, indeed, created it. The method was basic research; although it chiefly flourished in the faculties of arts and sciences, it reached out over the whole university, bringing great and swift improvement in professional standards throughout.

A special word should be said about the professional schools. At their best as integral parts of the complex university, they have improved their standards steadily in this century and are now regarded as the finest institutions of their kind in the world. The schools of medicine, law, and theology rest firmly upon substantial university studies in science, social science, and the humanities, and have succeeded in combining advancement of knowledge with the aim of producing competent physicians, lawyers, and ministers for the service of society. These schools were imbued with the instinct of practical usefulness to community, state, and nation, but it is the concept of basic research attained in a university context that gives them true stature. At the beginning of the century there were hardly a dozen institutions that deserved the title of university according to Flexner's definition, though many claimed it. There are now a hundred. The excellence of our universities has been in large part achieved by their devotion to the advancement of learning. Again quoting Flexner: "The truth is that specialization has brought us to the point we have reached, and more highly specialized intelligence will alone carry us further."[6]

The scientific method, which has proved so fruitful in research, has had a somewhat different result as it reached into the colleges, in its effects both on the content of the studies and on the methods of teaching. Extremely effective though the superb methods of scientific investigation have been in their original fields, they are often inappropriate and damaging when applied to areas of study that by their natures are less capable of precise measurement. This is true of many of the social sciences, which can never be genuine sciences. The scientific method is even more damaging when it is applied inappropriately and unskillfully to the humanities, as was the case when it influenced early literary study and later disturbed the metaphysical aspects of philosophy. Nevertheless, the rigorous research procedures of the natural sciences have had the effect of tightening the thinking and improving the tone and product of scholarship in most areas of knowledge. The scientific spirit is an atmosphere and is breathed in by all who deal in intellectual matters. It has penetrated and saturated the academic mind, and its virtues and faults are reflected in the attitudes, personalities, conduct, and characters of most professors. It has made them prize objectivity and impersonality, and appear to be neutral commentators on even the most moving topics. This state of mind has been best exhibited in the lecture hall where the student, perhaps curious about his professor's view of life, had few opportunities to ask questions or voice a different opinion. In spite of all the experimental approaches to the problems of the curriculum, the lecture became the characteristic method of teaching in the colleges in the third and fourth decades of this century; and when it was the sole or major mode of instruction, it contributed heavily to the deterioration of college teaching. Lately other forces have been at work here—the rapidly increasing numbers of students, the larger classes, the highly specialized training of teachers, the preoccupation of professors with narrow research projects, or their absence on missions for the government or the philanthropic foundations. In any case, beginning with the shift of emphasis by the sciences to the advancement of learning, the devotion to teaching has deteriorated during the century. The deterioration has been uneven: it is less in the humanities, greater in the social sciences, and greatest in the sciences. In their pursuit of research, scientists have tended to forget the less exciting duty of teaching. But very recently they have become alarmed at their failure to teach their subjects well, either to the students they hope to attract to the profession or to the intelligent students who do not plan to make a career of science.

The ideal of the advancement and transmission of knowledge in the universities has met another strong ideal native in America, the assumption that educational institutions should be useful to the society. The idea of service has its roots deep in the American soil. Benjamin Franklin had hoped that the university he wished to establish in Philadelphia (which later became the University of Pennsylvania) would be a practical institution for training students in commerce, agriculture, and science, in sharp contrast to the colonial colleges of New England and Virginia. And after Franklin, Thomas Jefferson had similar utilitarian ideas about his university at Charlottesville. The idea was behind the development of the Land Grant colleges and state universities, which have done such magnificent service to their localities. Unfortunately their very success made the universities vulnerable to all sorts of demands for the proliferation of special courses and "professional" schools for every vocation. Yet the ideal of service continues to flourish.

From the psychology of service to the community, it was a short step for higher education to make towards providing service to the nation when that service was required. The first notable step was taken when President Franklin Roosevelt called his Brain Trust into being during the depression. But that was only a prologue to the wide use of scholars during the Second World War. Indeed, the conclusion of the war might have been greatly delayed if the scientists and engineers, aided by refugee scientists from the totalitarian countries, had not perfected the nation's weapons for offense and defense. The social scientists too were most useful in the management of the war, and individuals in the humanities made their contribution. The academic man had become an essential participator and a major resource in American society.[7] But all this in turn was the beginning of an even greater involvement, the use the federal agencies now make, twenty years later, of the institutions of higher education for research and development in the physical sciences, research in biology and medicine, and in action for national welfare at home and abroad.

This involvement of higher education with the federal government has its salutary as well as its dangerous aspects. The facilities of many universities have been greatly increased and improved, and a new excitement in research has invigorated the campus. Moreover, individual professors' salaries have been much improved, to the benefit of all, and scientists and scholars have been drawn into the stream of world affairs. On the debit side there are the various imbalances created in the academic establishment by the presence of the government. We find an excessive concentration of research contracts in a few institutions; twenty-five universities receive four fifths of the funds. Also, within any single institution, the government's partiality for science has caused it to lavish funds on the sciences while the social sciences and, to an even greater extent, the humanities have been left with bare cupboards. The great attention to science may even do science itself a disservice, in the sense that here is research largely directed to a special end. The spirit of true research is freedom and spontaneity; it is an operation in which the scientist finds his way to an undesignated and possibly unexpected discovery; and it is the way in which the great imaginative advances have been made. In short, there is some danger in the situation by which the government, in pursuing its proper commitment to the security, health, and welfare of its citizens, creates these imbalances in educational institutions. The universities are deflected from their original free pursuit of new knowledge and tend to lose what would, if they could advance without the pressure of these external needs, be their own priorities of basic research.

As we look now at higher education with the perspective of history, we see that it has come a very long way in size, quality, and variety. Indeed, the diversity of the parts is in itself good, since more opportunities are provided for experiment. The present scene is highly disordered, but the confusion is evidence of abundant life and vigor. We are not inclined, I think, to demand order at the cost of freedom or to seek stability at the cost of growth. It would be well, however, if we were more aware of our direction and more certain of how to proceed. The new position of the United States in world affairs has relieved our educational provincialism and has caused many nations to look to us for leadership. Our culture has come to maturity in this century, and we no longer need to draw so deeply upon the intellectual capital of Europe. And yet it is certain that, while we have increased greatly the numbers of our scholars and scientists and have raised the general level of their intellectual competence and achievement, we have not yet produced our full share of seminal thinkers in many fields of learning.[8]

For the colleges, there remains the problem of shaping a program of studies—or indeed an educational plan—that will do for the student of today what the classical curriculum at its most vital, with its virtues of cohesiveness and discrimination, did for the student of an earlier time. The desideratum is to meet the needs of the modern world in content and method, and yet to preserve the proven values of twenty-five hundred years. This is, in effect, to construct a curriculum that will include in proper balance the old and the new—the timeless, liberal studies of literature, history, and philosophy and the tough-minded, empirical studies so useful at the present time, mathematics, the sciences, and the social sciences.

The graduate schools have still to solve the problems that rise from the fragmentation of knowledge, and there is a hopeful beginning in the interdisciplinary studies that have recently come into their programs. It is necessary for the health of all higher education that the graduate schools include in their aims the dedication to the dissemination as well as the advancement of learning, that in particular they rethink their position in the matter of preparing teachers for the nation's colleges. This will require a broader outlook, understanding and sympathy, and possibly some sacrifice of pride.

As for the leadership that will help to bring all these things about, more of the excellent people in the universities and colleges are needed who will extend their view beyond their devotion to their own work in their own fields to the large problems of higher education. The whole academic world needs to put its mind to the problem of leadership for the universities and colleges of the country. Those who are close to administration in higher education have begun to realize that perhaps our greatest need is academic statesmanship; for now, as always, without vision the people perish.

CHAPTER II | THE COLLEGE, 1900–1920

By the beginning of the twentieth century the direction of the development of the United States was confirmed. This country was to become an industrialized democracy on a huge scale. This development was still very much in progress, and by no means nearing completeness. There were vast areas of the country virtually uninhabited, and the balance was still a little in favor of agriculture as the prevailing mode of life in the nation. But the die was cast, and all the signs for the future pointed towards industry and commerce, conducted in large urban centers, as the major way of life.

The country had grown enormously in population and wealth since the Civil War, but the growth was uneven. The South was still exhausted and impoverished, and the West beyond the Mississippi was sparsely settled. Great tides of immigrants had come to the North to man the factories and mills, to build the cities and railroads, and to settle as farmers in the upper Middle West. Quantitatively, all the lines in the graph were straining upward, but the state of the nation was not healthy or easy. The wealth of the country was very inequitably distributed, not only regionally but individually. Great fortunes were being made from the railroads and the new industries, but the wealth was concentrated in the large cities of the East—New York, Boston, and Philadelphia. Society, too, had become stratified according to wealth and pretension, and the rich flaunted their status in the face of an offended and belligerent democracy. Individualism, properly called rugged, had by no means been tamed by egalitarianism, as it was to be in the years ahead. In politics, the country was officially conservative and moving rather blindly towards empire. On the surface the mood of the people was idealistic and optimistic, but the native idealism was being smothered under an overwhelming materialism, and the cheerful faith in progress and order was constantly being disrupted by untoward events and rebellious men. In the South there was a sullen torpor; in the West there was a mood of revolution in the agricultural and mining states; in the North labor was uneasy almost to the point of revolt. Radical thinking was rife, often to the point of anarchy. Even in religion the surface of fundamentalist orthodoxy was broken from time to time by ideas from the new science and the higher criticism of the Scriptures that reached this country from Europe.

In this seething world of change the American college of the first decade of the twentieth century was described as an island in time, as stagnant as a Spanish convent. This judgment was probably superficial, and certainly insufficiently sympathetic. The colleges, whether the independent and small ones in the country or the larger and new sort that were integral parts of their universities, faced many problems. They could often be classed with the undeserving poor—and there is no doubt that they were poor. The total income of all American colleges in 1900 was $35,084,000, and their total endowment $197,998,000; and these figures had only recently been achieved. In 1909, to take a year in the middle of the period we are considering, the endowment of Harvard, the wealthiest of the great universities, was $22,716,759, and the income from this source $966,113.[1] At the same time, the number of students had jumped in the last decade of the nineteenth century from 156,756 to 237,592, and by 1910 was to rise to 355,213. By 1920 the enrollments had risen to 597,880.[2] Further, the students who flooded the colleges at the beginning of the century were a new breed. It had become fashionable to go to college, and the students were wealthier and for the most part drawn from a different social class. They were predominantly Anglo-Saxon and middle-class, though a sprinkling of the children of recent immigrants began to appear—Irish, German, Jewish, Italian, Polish— and these students were often puzzled by or defiant of the monolithic society they had entered. There were, of course, many different kinds of students, even some "grinds" on the way to becoming teachers; but in general the classes were made up of the future owners and managers of the country, intent upon present social and athletic success before they entered the competitive world of which life in college was a miniature reflection. In the potpourri of the college population there were inevitably some sensitive and open-minded students, eager to learn, but for the most part minds were already made up, opinions and thoughts already shaped and hardened by social and family background. The students and the faculty faced each other like two opposing armies, hardly equal in numbers, but the faculty had a secret weapon in the dreaded markbook and could as a last resort banish the student from his Arcadia.

The collegiate world that the new students created and inhabited *was* a kind of coarse Arcadia. The faculty probably thought that the classroom and the courses, the teacher and the textbook, constituted college life, but most of the students were of a different opinion. The "real college life" of that early time has been vividly described by a perceptive and critical writer who lived in it, Henry Seidel Canby.[3] The students had created "a state within a state," a region where the sweater was of greater consequence than the gown. The college of Canby's time was a place where the two camps, students and faculty, saluted each other in passing and sometimes stopped for a chat. The "real" life of the students was an exceedingly competitive and strenuous preparation for the hurly-burly of life in America into which they were to graduate. Perhaps it was the remoteness of their college studies from contemporary relevance that, in part at least, encouraged the creation of an elaborate extracurricular life. "We were strenuous without thought to ask the reason why," says Canby:

For all but the congenitally lazy, the songful hours over beer steins, the country walks, and the midnights of intimate talk, were interludes (like our lessons) in a tense activity. The cry in our undergraduate world was always "do something," "what does he *do*?" Freshmen hurried up and down entry stairs seeking news for the college paper, athletes, often with drawn, worried faces, struggled daily to get or hold places on the teams, boys with the rudiments of business ability were managers of magazines, orchestras, teams, or co-operative pants-pressing companies. Those who had a voice sang, not for sweet music's sake, but to "make" the glee club. Long throats went in for social drinking, glib minds for politics; everything but scholarship was in my day an "activity," and called "doing something for the college." Fraternities read off each meeting night their record of successful achievements, where credit for study meant only that the brethren had kept out of trouble with the faculty. Brother Jones is left guard on the scrub; Brother Smith is "heeling" (expressive term) religion in the Y.M.C.A.; Brother Brown is being urged to write jokes for the Record; Brother Robinson is manager of the chess team. Some voice seemed always to be saying, "Work, for the night is coming." The toil was supposed to be fun, but the rewards were serious. No one that I remember did anything that was regarded as doing, for its own sake. No, the goal was prestige, social preferment, a senior society which would be a springboard to Success in Life. And all gilded, made into illusion, by the theory that in such strenuosity we demonstrated loyalty to our society, which was the college, that thus the selfish man transcended his egoistic self-seekings, and "did" something for Harvard, or Amherst, or Yale.[4]

Canby's description is drawn from Yale, at the time the darling college of America because of its athletic prowess. And there, indeed, the "real" collegiate life reached its highest development. But the scene was imitated by hundreds of colleges across the land. In tune with the country in that strenuous era, college presidents, almost with one accord, believed with Hadley of Yale that competition of any kind was good. It was a pity that the students did not compete strenuously in the intellectual aspects of their education, though it was pointed out to them that the word curriculum meant "race course." But in education the students got what they and the country wanted. This image of the college sank deep into the public consciousness and persists sixty years later, though it has been feminized by coeducation and made even more frivolous by Hollywood. The capital of this collegiate world, however, is no longer in the Northeast and the Ivy League, but has shifted to the West, Southwest, and South.

Big-time athletics, especially football, which had become the index in the public mind of the standing of the colleges, had already passed into a semiprofessional stage by 1905. The game was far too important to leave in the hands of the students. The old amateur coach—a graduate who, to help his college, had for a year or two delayed going into the bond business or his father's factory—gave way to the coach who was a professional and was paid for his work. Athletic programs of all kinds were expanded, the cost mainly paid by football receipts. New stadiums were built, and the game became big business. "Ringers" and "tramp athletes" moved from college to college as their services were required. Some men stayed in college or the professional school and continued to play football for five or six years—this in spite of the excessive roughness of the game. In 1905 the *Chicago Tribune* published statistics showing that 18 players had been killed and 159 seriously injured in the season that had just closed. A few colleges dropped football, to the alarm of President Theodore Roosevelt, who loved the game. He called the representatives of Harvard, Yale, and Princeton to a conference for the purpose of ameliorating brutality and foul play. The wedge and other dangerous tactics were eliminated, but it was not until 1911 that the game was opened up by the forward pass and the rule that gave a team four downs to make ten yards.[5] In these years baseball, track, and rowing (which had long histories) combined with football to provide spectacles for a sports-hungry public and, for the newspapers, copy in ever increasing quantity. It was still many years before the presidents of the colleges began to realize that they had allowed the genie to escape from the bottle.

At the beginning of the century, then, the students in the colleges had devised an educational system of their own—indeed, a culture, though hardly a civilization, made up of fraternities and clubs, sports and publications, with its own private values and rewards.[6] For the young men of the country it was a wonderful world. In 1909 Woodrow Wilson, then President of Princeton, could say of college life that "the side shows are so numerous, so diverting—so important, if you will—that they have swallowed up the circus."[7] In many respects, as I have said, the life the students made for themselves resembled the roaring, competitive life of the country beyond the college quadrangles; but in some respects it was better and preserved some native values that were fast disappearing from the life of the nation. Standards of value were more genuinely democratic and rested more on personal character and achievement than on wealth or social class. College life was touched with an idealism, a generosity, and a loyalty that were beyond that of the common life. Merriwell and Stover of Yale, its first citizens, were high-minded as well as ridiculous, and touchingly young.

In most colleges throughout the country at the turn of the century, the living conditions of the students were primitive, sometimes to the point of being barbarous. The older colleges of the East, modeled upon the English colleges, generally had some dormitory arrangements and a common dining hall. But the toilet facilities were in the basement; there was a pump in the yard, and water was taken to the rooms in pitchers and bottles—ammunition at hand for spring riots. With the greater numbers of students, however, the dormitory accommodations were outgrown. In many places fraternities were allowed to increase in number to supply the inadequacy, and in others the students obtained quarters for themselves in the neighborhood of the colleges. Occasionally, these were exclusive and palatial, shockingly so to the democratic public, as was the famous Gold Coast at Harvard. West of the Hudson, conditions were generally different. At Cornell, Michigan, Wisconsin, and the smaller colleges of the Midwest, the fraternities and sororities provided living quarters and meals. Students who were not in the fraternities were completely on their own, lived in boarding houses and rented rooms, or got their rooms for such services as stoking the furnace, and ate when and where they could. Waiting on table at student "eating joints" was the commonest form of helping to pay one's way through college. These haphazard arrangements were often owing to the poverty of the colleges, which had no funds for building dormitories; but they were often defended on ideational grounds, for the German conception of the proper nature of higher education prevailed in the universities.[8] As the education of women assumed greater proportions and importance, the necessity for looking after these students more carefully introduced a dormitory system in coeducational institutions that were still ideationally opposed to close supervision of the student's life. Cornell provided an example of this temper.

As the tide of Germanic influence ebbed after 1910, the older colleges of the Northeast set the pace in the movement to house virtually all of their students in dormitories. They saw that this was necessary if they were to preserve their character as compact educational communities. The movement was speeded by the feeling that freshmen ought to be protected from the sudden liberties of college life. There was also a less often mentioned desire on the part of the administration and faculty to give the student at an early stage a different and better conception of the purpose of a college education. President Lowell of Harvard counted the building of dormitories for half of his freshman class as one of his early triumphs.[9] But at Princeton, Wilson was thwarted in his quadrangle plan by the entrenched dining clubs. Before the First World War, as the wealth of the country increased, even the state universities gradually saw the advisability of housing their freshmen in dormitories owned and controlled by the institution; and the new buildings were generally in the architectural style known as Collegiate Gothic, a style that gave a name to the age. The fuller development of the dormitory movement was to come later in the century in the early thirties, when the elaborate "house" and "college" systems were established at Harvard and Yale, with each unit complete in itself with living quarters and common rooms, dining halls and libraries, under the supervision of a master and a number of fellows, some of them resident. The broader implication of the dormitory movement was that the American college was assuming the obligation of directing the social and moral aspects of the student's life as well as his educational development. It was in part also a reaffirmation of the English origins of the college in this country as opposed to the Germanic features of the university.

The old college of the late nineteenth century at its best had had a character of solidity and unity that produced a powerful, purposeful, and compact internal democracy that was much admired and imitated throughout the country. Through its methods of teaching—the recitation and the demonstration—it strove to train its students in mental discipline, and the hope of the college was to produce moral character rather than to instill knowledge or encourage curiosity. The small size of the classes studying a similar set of subjects, the customs of eight o'clock daily chapel, dormitory living, common activities, and athletic games assured the conscientious faculty that every student was known to his teachers and classmates. But this small isolated world could not last; it found itself increasingly out of touch with the life and thought of the country, unable to adapt itself with the required speed to the new demands of the time. It was possibly because they sensed this fact that the students had improvised a practical education of their own. The colleges themselves, far from being complacent, were struggling to create some kind of order out of the new conditions.

When the streams of new students came to the colleges at the turn of the century, they found that the colleges were not yet prepared to educate them, but were, to tell the truth, in a state of disorder unparalleled in their history. The elective system had triumphed almost everywhere, though a few citadels of the nineteenth-century college, such as Yale, Princeton, and many small denominational colleges, had not for a variety of reasons entirely capitulated. The trouble with the elective system was that it was no system at all. The set program of roughly common courses for all students had been invaded twenty-five years earlier by elective courses; these were offered first to upperclassmen, but by 1900 even the freshmen in many colleges were free to choose the courses they wanted. This was notably true of Harvard which, though not the inventor of the elective system, had under Eliot become its chief proponent. By 1900 the system had done its necessary work. Old areas of study had been subdivided into many subjects, and new subjects had been admitted to the curriculum. Under the spectacular advances of science, the old course called natural philosophy proliferated into the whole range of sciences as we know them today. Somewhat later, the old course in political economy was subdivided into several social sciences. Psychology, a new subject, had as its parents philosophy or "mental discipline" on one side and zoology on the other. These developments, of course, were essential to intellectual and educational health and progress and can hardly be regretted. The new materials and arrangements of knowledge allowed the student to proceed in sequence, depth, and thoroughness in a way that was impossible in the old general curriculum; and the way was opened to the specialization that was necessary in the new age.

In short, the elective system was admirably suited to make specialists and thus to lay the foundations for the universities that the country needed. The question was not whether to adopt the new learning, but rather how to adapt and manage the new studies so that they could appropriately and profitably be included in the existing colleges. In the first decade of the century, indeed, it was gravely questioned in some quarters whether there was any place left in the educational system for the American college as it had developed from its English origins. For a while it appeared that the colleges would be devoured by the aggressive professional schools and sloughed off by the rising universities. To some, Johns Hopkins, with its almost nonexistent undergraduate school, looked like an attractive model.

From the point of view of the colleges, the problem, then, was how to utilize wisely and discriminately the new freedom of choice in a wide range of subjects, without permitting the students to run wild. There can be no doubt that the undergraduate did misuse his freedom in the early phases of the elective system. The excellent students in the better colleges could be counted on to get a great deal out of their college years. But the indifferent and poor students who were in the vast majority took the easy and elementary courses, the popular lectures, and the convenient hours. Even the better students sought the spell-binding professor rather than the important subject of study. As the example of Harvard spread through all, or nearly all, of the larger colleges of the country, undergraduate scholarship declined steeply and probably reached its nadir about 1904–5. The professor, trained in Germany, employed the impersonal methods of that country—the lecture, the laboratory, the examination —and there was a minimum amount of contact between teacher and student. The seminar, another device from German education, was reserved for advanced graduate students; it was too expensive in time and money to be offered to undergraduates. Educationally, the rearrangements caused by the elective system were not very satisfactory to anybody, and the attitude of the busy student towards the faculty was still "educate me if you can." But the old curriculum had been even less exciting, and its dated methods of recitation in the exact words of the textbook were intolerable. Indeed, the old program of Greek, Latin, and mathematics, even spiced as it had come to be by English literature, history, and a few other subjects, seemed worlds away from the life the students were preparing to lead, and saw their parents leading, in American business, industry, and politics.

The impact of the elective system, then, even upon the most stable and strong colleges, was staggering. But it is necessary to insist that, though these colleges were disorganized, they were not indifferent. The sense of educational direction in the colleges was so weak as to be almost nonexistent. Yet they were concerned and, if they appeared to the candid observer to be stagnant, it was rather because they were paralyzed by indecision.[10] Behind the indecison there was little complacency as the faculties tried device after device to improve the state of things. In 1901 the College Entrance Examination Board was established, mainly upon the initiative of President Butler of Columbia, and the independent colleges of the East one by one adopted the examinations as a means of controlling the numbers and quality of applicants for admission. A serious and persistent attempt was made to articulate the work of the secondary schools with that of the colleges—an effort that after a few years became an unbearable tyranny over the schools as the colleges prescribed specific subjects and even the books to be mastered by the candidates. Few men and women who went to Eastern colleges before the First World War can forget *Silas Marner* and Burke's *Speech on Conciliation*. In the West the high-school certificate continued to be the means of admission to college, though students so admitted were soon dropped by the hundreds. In the more advanced colleges, old honors programs were refurbished and new ones invented, but small incentive was provided for the student to undertake them. There was little sense of competition under the elective system, in which each student was going his separate way. In the West it was enough for the student to stay in college as the mortality rate rose to 50 percent. In the East the current ideal was the "gentleman's C." In all regions it was the common boast of the student that he "never cracked a book."

Nevertheless, with so much earnestness and persistence on the part of the faculties of the colleges, it was inevitable that conditions should begin to improve. The first honors here must go to Princeton. Woodrow Wilson, elected to the presidency of Princeton in 1902, the same year as Butler at Columbia, soon began to formulate and put into operation his preceptorial plan. He brought to Princeton fifty promising young scholars to teach the undergraduates in small discussion groups associated with their courses—a significant achievement in promoting respect for scholarship. To Bryn Mawr, it seems, must go the honor of being the first college to arrange the new materials of learning into group requirements of courses. Embryonic systems of majors and minors began to appear in a number of colleges, assuring some degree of thoroughness and depth in the student's learning. Then, upon his inauguration as President of Harvard in 1909, Lowell abandoned the elective system and set up instead a system of distribution and concentration in the curriculum, which has become the practice now followed in most colleges.[11] It was a momentous event in the educational world, marking the end of an era and the beginning of a new one. Much remained to be done in the way of refinement and development, and the end is not yet; but the first step had been taken in the long journey towards a modern curriculum that would do for contemporary America what the old classical curriculum had done for the eighteenth century.

A further word of explanation on the developing new arrangements may be useful. The system of distribution assured the faculty that the student would become acquainted with the fundamental areas of knowledge, and it distinguished for the student the subjects most central to his education and important for his educational purposes later in his college career, and possibly in graduate or professional school. The system of concentration gave the college a task and a purpose of its own, distinct at least for the time from the graduate and professional school. For the student it provided an educational depth and a junior mastery that the laissez faire of uncontrolled election could not achieve. These arrangements gave a sense of direction to collegiate education that it had lacked since the triumph of the elective system. Gradually the old three-year programs by which the colleges had in effect admitted their lack of a goal were eliminated, and so, too, were the combined programs with the professional schools that had threatened the colleges with inconsequence. As Lowell had hoped, it now appeared that the colleges were "worth saving."

It is clear that, as the years moved towards the entry of the United States into the First World War, the whole nature of student life began to improve. The curriculum, as we have seen, became infinitely richer and more relevant and was on the way to even better things. The studies began to engage the interest of the undergraduate. Academic scholarship improved materially in the second decade of the century, as new and better methods of instruction came into use and tutorial guidance, preceptorial classes, and seminars supplemented the lectures and laboratories. Moreover, college life itself gradually became more civilized. The barbarous hazing and the rough class fights had been tamed in most colleges and had been eliminated altogether in some. By 1915 no fewer than 123 institutions had adopted some form of an honor system, and student government had been established in many colleges. Manners were becoming milder. Student interests had begun to broaden and become more intellectual. In a number of colleges a new literary and artistic movement took hold, and this could be seen vividly at work in such colleges as Yale and Harvard, and a little later at Princeton. George Wilson Pierson discusses this movement at Yale in a chapter called "The Literary Renaissance" in his history of the College.[12] Within a few years in the second decade of the century there were present at Yale a group of men who were to become significant figures in the cultural life of the country. Among them were Archibald MacLeish, Stephen Vincent Benét, Thornton Wilder, Philip Barry, Walter Millis, Wilmarth Lewis, Henry Luce, and Britten Hadden. Cole Porter, Douglas Moore, Quincy Porter, and Reginald Marsh added luster from other fields. The same ferment was going on at Vanderbilt, with an emphasis of its own, and there were comparable movements in many colleges across the country. All this meant that the American colleges were on the way towards mastering many of their problems, though much remained to be done. By 1917 genuine progress had been made towards making the college a civilized and more scholarly community, and as the students left the campus for the battlefield, the administration and faculty could look forward with hope for further progress after the war.

The faculty of a college in the first decades of the century was likely to be made up of a considerable variety of personalities and minds. As survivors of an earlier age, there lingered into the new century many older teachers who taught in the rigid, outmoded method of recitation and thought the heart of education was in disci-

pline and memory. Other survivors from a quieter world were present, too, professors of an older humanism, of vast learning and
culture, and often men of letters themselves, but with little of the
paraphernalia of the new professional scholarship. Their prototype
was Emerson; his descendants were such men as Henry Augustin
Beers, Caleb Winchester, John Bascom, and John Erskine, to name
only a few. Also on the scene were men who would be great minds
in any age, such as William James at Harvard, Willard Gibbs at
Yale, J. H. Breasted at Chicago, and Franz Boas at Johns Hopkins,
but some of them unappreciated by their contemporaries. Here and
there, too, could be found whole galaxies of men of large and lasting
influence, such as the brilliant department of philosophy at Harvard;
and then there were powerful individual teachers who were able to
disturb the complacency of tough-minded students or shock their
colleagues by dealing frankly with matters of immediate relevance.
Such men were Woodrow Wilson of Princeton and William Graham
Sumner of Yale. Another group in the faculty of any large college
was likely to be made up of men trained in Germany and deeply
committed to German techniques of scholarship and specialization.
They taught subjects rather than students and yearned for the time
when the college would become a university. The undergraduate
courses they taught were likely to be the first courses in a sequence
that inevitably led to the doctor's degree. Finally, in almost every
college there were one or more enthusiastic teachers who lectured to
the undergraduates with enormous gusto, if with no lasting effect,
and frequently also to clubs in the outside world; they also wrote easy
books to improve the thin culture of the country.[13] It was this last
kind of professor that the nostalgic alumni, buried deep in mundane
affairs, remembered. But even though the faculty changed its personnel slowly, there was in the second decade evidence of an increase in
serious, thoughtful, and enlightened teaching.

These, then, were the individual members of the college faculty;
but they seldom operated any longer as a corporate unit, as they had
done earlier. In a few colleges the faculty still had power and exer-

cised an authority reminiscent of the nineteenth century. But the pressures on teachers were numerous and varied, and the strain caused the faculty to disintegrate as a single body. The deeper cause, however, was the rise of the university with its effect of dividing the faculty into departments. The loyalty that was once given to the institution as a whole began to shift to the departments, for through the departments preferment and salary came. The faculty was, also, further removed from the president, who had delegated his powers to the dean. In the larger and more complex institutions, matters once debated by the whole faculty gradually came to be decided by committees; indeed, government by committee became a general practice. The college at Columbia University was an early and symptomatic representative of this development. With the progress of the faculty member depending more and more upon his published work and the favor of his department, it is little wonder that the faculty meetings were poorly attended and the affairs of the college left in the hands of the dean and his committees.

In a materialistic society that measured a man's value by his income, it was inevitable that the professor would be little esteemed. Socially, in those early days of the century he ranked a little lower than the parson and the physician, and perhaps a little higher than the dentist. In some of the older college centers, the faculty wives looked down their noses at men in business and trade, but in the public mind the teacher was infinitely below the financial men, the political figures, and the lawyers who now began to be a majority in the college's board of trustees. At the same time, it was the age of characters in the college faculty, and many a college had powerful personalities who were quite capable of holding their own with the great men of affairs. Unfortunately, the two worlds seldom met, and when they did there was disagreement and embarrassment as the conversation got into the dangerous areas of politics or economics. To the professor the businessman was usually a barbarian, limited to immediate and mundane matters and lacking a true sense of values;

to the man of business the teacher was an impractical person who would have starved in the real world, and who spent his life on trivialities in the company of adolescents. It was to take a devastating depression and some spectacular achievements in the Second World War to alter for the better the popular conception of the professor. Yet even now the intellectual is often contemptuously dismissed as an egg-head.

Unfortunately for the teacher, the college always depends upon the material good estate of the world of business and industry; and the first two decades of the twentieth century were not generally prosperous times. In 1909, to take a year in the middle of the period we are considering, Harvard, the wealthiest of our universities, spent a total of $944,649 in salaries for the whole university. The full professor received at most $4,000 a year. By 1918 matters had improved, and the official Harvard figures were as follows: professor, $4,000–5,500; associate professor, $3,500; assistant professor, $2,500–3,000; instructor, $1,000–2,000.[14] Even with the dollars of those days, the salaries were hardly princely, and if they were low at Harvard they were almost negligible at the small denominational colleges of the South and West. The salaries at the state colleges, carefully watched by the legislatures, were not as generous as those at Harvard. Moreover, promotion at all colleges was slow, and it often took fifteen years or more for the teacher to attain his professorship. Further, until Andrew Carnegie set up his pension system for teachers in 1905, the professor had nothing to look forward to upon retirement. As an extra turn of the screw, teachers in denominational colleges were excluded from the Carnegie plan. The prospect of starting a career in teaching and scholarship on a salary of $1,200 to $1,500, after an arduous professional training, was not very enticing to proud and cultured men, and the wonder is that the colleges found so many able and devoted men and women to enter such an exacting life.

Although this aspect of higher education will be dealt with at greater length when the universities are considered, some observations must be made here on the trustees and the administration of the colleges, the gods who rule this nether world. The immediately striking fact is that by 1900 the larger colleges, especially those that were parts of universities, were rapidly coming under secular control. The boards of trustees or regents were beginning to be dominated by lawyers and businessmen, though here and there vestiges of the older clerical control might still be seen. This development was advantageous to the colleges whose larger endowments and properties, to say nothing of their more complex problems, needed expert care. At any rate, it was entirely consonant with the temper of the country at the time. The small independent or denominational colleges, however, were more conservative and slower to take this step. In the East the alumni whose loyalty had been so thoroughly nourished by college rivalries now pushed their way into the management of the much loved college. In the West the state colleges had always been more secular and were naturally under the control of the important businessmen of the state and of the legislatures that controlled the purse. The main advantage of such secular control of the boards of trustees was in the gathering and management of financial resources, both of which were badly needed. But there were disadvantages. The alumni were not always wise in the exercise of their powers and were frequently more interested in the athletic standing of the college than in its intellectual integrity and purpose. The businessmen sometimes endangered academic freedom by trying to run the college as if it were an industry, and they were inclined to look upon the faculty as employees whose opinions should coincide with their own. Indeed, the records show that the first years of the new century were stormy ones in the matter of academic freedom. Without the secular interest the colleges would certainly have been financially poorer; with it they were frequently uncomfortable.

As the composition of the boards of trustees changed and the affairs of the colleges became more complex, it was natural that the president chosen by a board should be, if not one of themselves, at least no longer a clergyman, who could hardly be expected to comprehend, much less to appreciate, the immense material progress of industry and business. The clergy, too, had suffered loss of stature in the American mind from the effects of the new science and the higher criticism of the Scriptures. The boards increasingly turned away from the clergy for their presidents; and the striking personalities and notable achievements of laymen like Eliot, Gilman, and White in the preceding generation had confirmed them in their confidence in the trend. Then, too, the state universities, which often had the reputation of being irreligious, had always drawn presidents from their own faculties or from the world of affairs. At any rate, by 1905 the larger colleges of the East all had secular presidents, and a remarkable group of men they were. At Harvard Eliot continued to be president until 1909 and then was succeeded by Lowell, a political scientist; at Yale Hadley, an economist, was president; a philosopher, Butler, ruled Columbia; Wilson, a political scientist, was president at Princeton; and at Cornell Schurman, a diplomat, was at the head of the university.

The old college president who found time to know all the students and to teach a class of seniors had disappeared. With the greater size and complexity of the institution, Parkinson's Law began to operate. Discipline was delegated to the dean, a new official in American colleges; ceremonies and correspondence and most public affairs were put in the care of the secretary; educational policy was managed by faculty committees; a new breed of counselors was created to care for the personal and educational needs of the students. The president was on the road, extolling or explaining his college and begging money. Much later, if he could manage it, he was to delegate money-raising to a new office of development. The president of the new age became a remote figure to the undergraduate; but since it was an honored tradition, the students usually made him into a legend of lovable eccentricity if he gave them the chance, and they followed his activities on the national scene with loyal pride. His triumphs were theirs, too.

In summary, we may say that the indecision and apparent stagnation of the American college, caused primarily by the conflict of the old classical curriculum and the elective system, disappeared in the early years of the twentieth century. Almost everywhere the old curriculum was changed beyond recognition. Greek was no longer a requirement for entrance, and Latin, though still often required for entrance and for the B.A., was clearly doomed to the same fate. New curriculums stressing science, the social sciences, and modern languages were offered as optional ways to the bachelor's degree. The curriculum of the college was made richer and more interesting. By 1910 the elective system in its absolute freedom had run its course, and in its place the colleges had set up group requirements for breadth and rudimentary major and minor programs for concentration. Though incomplete and undeveloped, the ground plan to be realized later in the century began to be visible. Along with the new programs of study, new methods of instruction were adopted by the faculty and recitation and demonstration were largely abandoned. Entrance standards were gradually improved after the establishment of the College Entrance Examination Board, and better students, better prepared, sought the colleges. As a consequence of all these events, undergraduate scholarship began to attain higher levels of performance after 1905. There was no diminution in the number of extracurricular activities, to be sure, but they were probably better managed and less emphasized. In the second decade of the century, it became clear that the college world had broadened its cultural interests remarkably, and the quality of student life had improved. The living conditions of the students now began to be a matter of concern to the colleges, as was the task of counseling, both personal and academic. If the colleges were not yet the equivalent of the

English universities in the quality of their education, they were not going to become German Gymnasien, as it had seemed for a while they might.

Along with all the changes and improvements, the colleges also suffered some deleterious developments. Because of the enormous expansion of knowledge and the degree of specialization needed to cope with it, the faculty as a corporate body developed a tendency to disintegrate into departments at an accelerating pace, a development that resulted in the faculty's loss of much of its control over its own affairs. The trend was most apparent in those institutions that were at the time in the process of building a university structure of graduate and professional schools. The younger teacher looked to the department for his appointment and advancement instead of to the college, and the resources of the college were almost invariably siphoned off to support the new university development. The increasingly secular boards of trustees and presidents found the departmental structure much easier to control, and the tidy organization pleased their sense of order.

This, then, was the general condition of the colleges in 1917. When the country went to war with imperial Germany, the colleges were suddenly emptied as students volunteered for military service. In the following year, the campuses were made military camps for underage students newly come from the schools. An era had ended. When the students came back to college in the fall of 1919, they sensed that they were entering a different world.

CHAPTER III | GRADUATE AND PROFESSIONAL
SCHOOLS BEFORE
THE FIRST WORLD WAR

The rise and development of the university in the United States during the last one hundred years has been almost as spectacular as the rise of the German universities in the nineteenth century. Of course there was a close connection between the two events, though the differences were considerable. The thousands of young American scholars returning from their training in German universities during the latter half of the nineteenth century brought with them the continental idea of a university—which was essentially that the primary function of the university was the discovery and advancement of knowledge. There was no American idea of a university sufficiently alive and advanced to counter this single-minded conception. As we have seen, in the closing decades of the nineteenth century the colleges were paralyzed between the inadequacies of the old curriculum and the chaos of the elective system, and were inundated by the inrush of a new and different student body. Most of the colleges had neither the resources nor the will to do anything new and daring. It was clear that the country after the Civil War needed professionally trained people in many fields to confront the new conditions of an increasingly industrialized democracy; and it was equally clear that the German model, however admirable in its purity and useful in its ultimate results, was not capable of meeting all the needs of this country.

What our society did have to meet the continental idea of a university was a strong native pragmatism and a sharp sense of adaptation and inventiveness. The country had fitted the English college to its own purposes, and now in the late nineteenth century it would do a comparable thing to the German idea. The result was an American institution of immense variety, as we shall see when we look at a few typical universities in some detail. But for all their variety, there was one common element in these institutions, which set them off from the continental university. Where the German university was dedicated to scholarship and research, the new American universities were intent upon service to their region or the country. However pure the scholarly idea of the university was at its inception, say at Johns Hopkins in 1876 or Chicago in 1890, the American university soon saw that its first task in the twentieth century would be to train the professionals the country demanded. And the country wanted professionally trained men and women in almost every reasonably respectable vocation; it was not content with the traditionally learned professions of divinity, medicine, and law. In our egalitarian society all vocations were equal, and if ministers of the gospel needed a professional school for their training, so, too, did businessmen; and journalism was as worthy a profession as the law.

What we see, then, as we look at the educational scene in the United States as the nineteenth century drew to a close is the new university responding eagerly to the needs of the people as the old college had not done since the eighteenth century and was not yet capable of doing again. And the new necessities were those of a rising, wealthy, complex society on the way to becoming highly industrialized, egalitarian and pragmatic in its thinking, intensely progressive, and beginning to assume an imperial position among the nations. To meet the conditions of the time and to steer the new universities through the vast expansion of knowledge, especially in the areas of the burgeoning sciences and social sciences, the times were provided with some remarkable educators. These were such men as Eliot of Harvard, Gilman of Johns Hopkins, White of Cornell, and Harper of Chicago—three of them, surprisingly, associated with Yale College, which at the time was the citadel of the older order and a most reluctant participant in the university movement. They were the great pioneers, but by 1900 their work had mainly been done, though their influence was still strong. Each of these men had been the architect of a distinctive university, each institution differing from the others in detail and personality.

By the beginning of the new century, however, a rough similarity had developed among all the universities. There was a central core of the arts and sciences, usually consisting of a college and a graduate school; grouped about the center were the professional schools that the particular university wished to emphasize, usually schools of divinity, medicine, and law in the older universities of the East, but in many cases, especially in the West, without the theological school and with many other professional schools to fill any supposed gap. Moreover, the new universities were much alike in being intensely secular institutions with men of affairs or scholars trained in Germany as presidents, instead of the clergymen of the old college. The new universities were likewise intensely professionalized in the personnel of their faculties in contrast to the widely cultured teachers of the earlier time; and finally the whole university was rigidly departmentalized as knowledge expanded and learning became fragmented. In truth, the new university seldom had a common faculty; it had instead a series of divisions and departments, and the departments were arranged in a hierarchy of ranks, a relatively new device in the American educational world. By 1900 the pattern of the American university had been fairly set, and the organization had begun to harden into a form that was a close adaptation of a complex and sophisticated business firm. It had come so far from the original model as to be almost a native invention. It was supported by wealthy alumni or the state; it was managed by lay experts in administration; its employees were research specialists; and it produced not only the experts of the future, but also innumerable books and articles.

At this point it would be well to look at a few of the new university establishments as they stood in the first decade of the twentieth century. They fall into certain types. The first is the university raised upon the foundation of an old and distinguished college, and in this kind I shall consider Harvard and Yale. The second is the new university created in the nineteenth century out of whole cloth, and here I shall deal with Johns Hopkins and the University of Chicago. The third is the university that developed out of the state educational institutions, and here I wish to speak of the University of Michigan and the University of Wisconsin. The selection of these universities, typical though they are of aspects of the university movement in this country, is somewhat arbitrary, and I am conscious of doing some injustice to other rising universities, such as Pennsylvania, Princeton, Cornell, Minnesota, Illinois, California at Berkeley, North Carolina, Tulane, and Vanderbilt, among still others. A brief comment upon Columbia will be made at the end, for in several respects it was the most complex of all the universities of the time. When in 1900 the leading universities of the country banded together in a new organization, the Association of American Universities, there were approximately thirty members, and all of those mentioned above were included.

By the first decade of the present century, Harvard had become the foremost of America's universities.[1] It was not only the oldest of our educational institutions; it was also the wealthiest. It had achieved its eminence as a university in spite of a reluctance on the part of loyal graduates of the College. But Charles William Eliot was a powerful man and was frequently right, indeed often insufferably so. His espousal of the elective system for the college had opened the way to the full development of Harvard as a university, and Eliot had furthered the movement by his intentional mingling of undergraduate and graduate instruction, the binding element being the subject to be learned rather than the students who made up the class. The method of instruction was mainly the lecture and the laboratory, with the seminar reserved for advanced graduate work and the dissertation and examination concluding the whole. It was in effect the procedure of the German universities transferred to the American scene and conducted largely by professors trained abroad. In this concentrated drive on Harvard's part to become the country's greatest university, the fortunes of Harvard College in 1904–5 reached their lowest point. But the graduate school flourished to such an extent that, in spite of the assault of William James on the Ph.D.,[2] by the first decade of this century Harvard had become the largest producer of advanced degrees in the country, which was now training its own professors in ever increasing numbers.

Undoubtedly it was the adoption of the elective system that gave Harvard the necessary freedom to develop the university idea, and the proliferation of departments as knowledge expanded that provided the opportunity. In Eliot's regime, which lasted until 1909, and in A. Lawrence Lowell's tenure as president, the greatness of Harvard lay in the eminence of the faculty rather than in superior organization. One remembers Harvard's great departments of philosophy, history, English, the ancient and modern literatures, mathematics, and the sciences before the First World War. The scholars and scientists who made up these distinguished departments were drawn from all parts of the civilized world, and Harvard became recognized abroad as one of the great educational institutions of the twentieth century. Along with the growth in strength and quality of the university's personnel, there was a proportionate increase in library and laboratory resources. At the same time, though with many setbacks and hesitations, the standards of the work required of students improved. This strong movement towards pre-eminence in the faculty of arts and sciences at Harvard was immensely fortified by the proliferation and improvement of a long list of professional schools and research institutes. The quality of the law and medical faculties brought special acclaim to the university. As the First World War came to be a reality to the United States rather than the sound of distant guns, there was little doubt in the public mind that Harvard was the foremost of America's universities, and this position she has continued to hold to the present, though perhaps with less margin than formerly.

The tortuous and reluctant progress of Yale to the status of a great university is illustrative of many aspects of the history of the country in the nineteenth and twentieth centuries.[3] There had always been eminent men on the Yale faculty, and by 1861 she had acquired many features of a university. Not only had Yale in that year awarded the first degrees of doctor of philosophy earned in the United States, but she already had professional schools of theology, medicine, and law. Her interest in science, which was a powerful instrument towards university reform, had been evident in the Sheffield Scientific School, and there were strong departments in such diverse fields as chemistry, geology, anthropology, and linguistics. As early as 1856 James Dwight Dana had a vision of Yale as "the Great American University," but in the nineteenth century in New Haven the movement did not develop much further. The truth was that Yale was too fond of the great college and of the collegiate way of life. The administration, and much of the faculty, felt that in a precipitate joining of the university movement Yale had too much to lose. As a consequence, when Noah Porter, a clergyman and a strong College man, was elected president in 1871, the College was reconfirmed, and the men at Yale with strong predilections for the university idea, Gilman and White and later Harper, went elsewhere to build the new universities of the country. It was characteristic of Yale that in her instructional procedures she should insist upon the separation of the undergraduates and the graduate students. Only very recently, under great pressure for early specialization in some areas of learning, have the two groups begun to meet in the same classes.

It was not until the drastic reform of 1919, when the power was lodged in the University instead of the College, that the way was opened at Yale for the full development of the university idea. Then in the following decade, under the presidency of James Rowland Angell, Yale made a strenuous and successful effort to regain her place as one of America's foremost institutions of higher education by building her graduate and professional schools into first-rate parts of a modern university. This is best seen in the older professional schools of law, medicine, and divinity; but the change is also apparent in such smaller schools of the university as forestry, the drama, fine arts, and music.

A second group of institutions that emerged as universities late in the nineteenth century was made up of those which had no collegiate past, but were created first as universities. As representatives of this group I have chosen Johns Hopkins University, which opened its doors in 1876, and the University of Chicago, which began to operate in 1892. The foundings of these institutions were events of momentous importance in the history of higher education in the United States. If these two universities had not been founded, and had not added their special points of view, American higher education in the twentieth century would have had a very different history.

Johns Hopkins was the first of the new universities to make pure scholarship its chief ideal.[4] Daniel Coit Gilman was the president engaged by the trustees to develop a great graduate university upon the German model. In the choice of Gilman, Hopkins was most fortunate, for they had selected one of the great educational statesmen of the time. From the beginning Gilman's primary concern was to assemble a distinguished faculty, and in this he was eminently successful. He created in Baltimore an institution that was unique in its spirit of professional research. The faculty remained the center of the university. As one would expect from the spirit of the time as well as from Gilman's background in the Sheffield Scientific School at Yale, he emphasized the sciences, where the new truths for the betterment of mankind were to be found. He raided American colleges and universities for excellent scholars and scientists and brought distinguished men from abroad as visiting professors. And this fresh and free spirit was to influence the whole fabric of higher education. It was the opinion of Eliot at Harvard that graduate education did not thrive in this country until Johns Hopkins set an example for other universities, including Harvard, to follow.

But if the faculty was excellent, it was no more so than the students who flocked to the university for their graduate training. Johns Hopkins was the first university to use fellowships in a systematic way to recruit graduate students, and from the beginning an outstanding group of carefully selected men chose to pursue their studies at Hopkins rather than follow the crowd to Germany or go to an older institution in the United States. Among the students there were such men of stature as Woodrow Wilson, Walter Hines Page, Josiah Royce, Abraham Flexner, and Herbert Baxter Adams. By the beginning of the twentieth century, Hopkins had been surpassed by Harvard as the greatest producer of doctoral degrees, but far into the century many a college and university faculty was staffed by distinguished professors who had received their advanced training at Johns Hopkins.[5]

Besides providing a model for the development of the university idea and teachers for many faculties, Johns Hopkins did other things that made for the professional consciousness of the modern university. Hopkins has been called "the cradle of the scholarly journal in America," and the number of its periodicals was only surpassed in number by the University of Chicago at a later time. Though a "university press" had been established at Cornell in 1869 to provide a workshop for its students in journalism, the credit should go to Hopkins for founding in 1891 the first true university press devoted to the advancement of learning. In this as in many matters the example of Hopkins was soon followed by the other universities. But after 1900 the standing of Hopkins as the most interesting and influential of American universities began to decline. The causes were several: the university idea had been adopted by other institutions; the money to support the university was insufficient, and new funds had not been found; the immense reputation the Hopkins medical school had achieved overshadowed the university as a whole, and probably siphoned off prospective financial support. In any judgment, however, Hopkins had earned the gratitude of everyone interested in higher education and has attained a distinguished place in the history of American university development.

Like a relay runner, the University of Chicago, which began its operation in 1892, took the baton from Johns Hopkins in the development of the university idea in America.[6] Hopkins had been the great pioneer in the movement; Chicago now was to be the mature embodiment of the idea, the pattern and model for the university of twentieth-century America. The fundamental policy of the new university was announced by its first president, William Rainey Harper: "It is proposed in this institution to make the work of investigation primary, the work of giving instruction secondary." Promotion of faculty members at Chicago was dependent upon publication. Further, the university, in addition to such novel arrangements as a quarter system, a lower or collegiate college for the first two years, and a university college for the last two, had all the appurtenances and emphases that we have now come to take for granted in a modern university. From the beginning the pride of the university was in its graduate and professional divisions. No sooner had the university opened in 1892 than a university press was established. No sooner was the faculty assembled and rigorously departmentalized than the university became the sponsor and publisher of a multitude of learned journals, most of them in the sciences, but all illustrating the importance of research and the specialization of knowledge in all fields. Moreover, to a degree hitherto unknown in American higher education, the faculty was arranged in a hierarchy, with three kinds of professors of permanent rank at the top and five grades of people with one-year appointments at the bottom. There were also, of course, grades between. Indeed, the whole university was organized as completely and as tightly as a large American business, and the personnel of the institution was intensely professionalized. Endowed by the new industrial wealth so characteristic of the time and the country, and established in the heart of America, the university was also endowed with a spirit equally native and timely. From the beginning the temper of the university was dynamic and aggressive, inventive and experimental, and yet at the same time pious in a liberal sense and dedicated to serving the country through learning and action. In the three quarters of a century since its founding, Chicago has been remarkably consistent in holding to its ideal.

The man who made the University of Chicago what it was illustrates superbly the value and power of the individual in shaping the history of an institution, and indeed of a whole era. This was William Rainey Harper, who at the age of thirty-two held three professorships at Yale. His first great achievement after he became President of Chicago was his astonishing extraction of $35 million for endowment from John D. Rockefeller, and land valued at several millions from Chicago businessmen. Possibly in 1890 Rockefeller had not developed the finesses of philanthropy that he later employed, but it is clear that Harper was not required to match the grant. He surprised the philanthropist by his endless requirements for buildings and professors, but in time Rockefeller was to say that he had never made a better investment. An even greater achievement, perhaps—one requiring qualities beyond ambition, energy, and imagination—was Harper's success in assembling a faculty worthy of the great university that Chicago was to be. His budget provided for 80 professors, but after a journey to the East he found himself with 120. The faculty he finally assembled included eight former presidents of institutions, five professors from Yale, fifteen professors from Clark (twelve of whom were biologists), and men in lower ranks from these places and elsewhere. When the university opened its doors in October 1892, students flocked in from every part of the country and from foreign lands. It is notable that the number of graduate students, 210, and the number of divinity students, 204, together outnumbered the undergraduates, 328, in the new university.

With the success of the University of Chicago in the early decades of the century, it was clear that the form and spirit of the university in the United States had been set. There were, and are, differences in details, of course, but the emphasis upon research and publication had been confirmed; the professional spirit of the faculty was woven deeply into the fabric of the university; the organization was fixed into ranks and functions; and the whole system of higher education was directed to the service of society. The democratic and progressive heartland of America had been endowed by new and native wealth with a university that matched the older universities of the East in power and influence, and expressed better than they the character and will of the people.

The third group of universities, which emerged strongly in the first two decades of the present century, was the state universities. To represent this group I have chosen the universities of Michigan and Wisconsin. It was a temptation to choose Cornell here because of its excellence and the influence it had on the universities in the West, but the very features of Cornell that Carl Becker so eloquently and justly praised militated against its representative qualities—the fact that Cornell was both a public and a private university, that it looked both East and West, and that it had a special personality of its own, which transcended its location.[7] Michigan and Wisconsin were more characteristic of their region and had their greatest flowering in the period we are now considering. Both of them, moreover, showed traces of the elements that entered into the establishment and history of the typical state university—the Jeffersonian design of the University of Virginia, the purposes of the Jacksonian democratization, the missionary zeal of such Eastern institutions as Yale and Princeton, the rejuvenating effect of the Land Grant Acts of 1862 and 1890, and finally the powerful influence of the continental universities. But whatever the influences, a strong native instinct modified the universities of Michigan and Wisconsin to suit home uses as they struggled to meet the crude and stubborn anti-intellectualism of the time. The fact that they succeeded so admirably enhances the credit due them. It may be noted that they acquired the name of university well before they were such in fact, but in that they were typically American.

If Henry Philip Tappan had been able to have his way at Michigan in 1852, there would have been the beginnings of a great university at Ann Arbor on the German model at that time.[8] He hired a faculty of some distinction and soon established a scientific division like those of Yale and Harvard. In 1858 the university offered master's degrees in arts and in the sciences, but was able to attract few students. Tappan was more successful in introducing the idea that the University of Michigan should become the head and special director and caretaker of the educational system of the state, an idea that in the hands of James B. Angell, the institution's greatest president, was to become the special glory of the university. In the catalogue of the University of Michigan for 1853–54, we find Tappan's statement of his aims: "The System of Public Instruction adopted by the State of Michigan is copied from the Prussian, acknowledged to be the most perfect in the world. . . . In the University, it is designed to organize all the Faculties with the exception of the Theological, which will be left to the different denominations."

But in the mid-nineteenth century, Michigan was little more than a small and inferior college, and Tappan's hope of a great university in Ann Arbor was a false dawn. In 1863 he was relieved of the presidency because Michigan could not accept his German ideal of scholarship for its own sake. What was desired by the state was a training much more immediately and clearly practical and vocational. It was not until Johns Hopkins had introduced the new spirit into the educational world, and Angell had caught that spirit, that Michigan began to attain the status of a true university, dedicated to the search for truth. And even then the pure ideal was tempered by the ideal of direct service to the state which the federal and state governments are prone to fasten upon universities, then and now.

The idea Angell developed at the University of Michigan was that the state owed it to its citizens to provide higher education for all.

If democracy was to succeed, higher education was a necessity; and the state university should become the defender of democracy, its safeguard in a greedy time against avarice and unequal treatment. Angell became the leader and spokesman for the rising state universities. What Michigan did under its successive presidents was to organize the educational system of the state with the university as its head. Admission to the university was made by certificate, and close relations with the secondary schools were cultivated. By its attention to the high schools, the university was able to direct elementary and secondary public education, and was thus able to free itself from the subcollegiate work that had been a responsibility of its college. This allowed the university to devote its resources to its proper purposes. The arrangements provided a sound workable system of public education and brought great friendliness and appreciation to the university from the citizens, who felt that the institution in Ann Arbor was their university. Moreover, standards were raised all around. Other states in the Midwest and the Far West observed what Michigan had done and followed her example.

Angell's idea that higher education should be free and available to all was widely adopted and, indeed, is much alive today. There were strong objections, however, from several expected quarters. At home, there was opposition from the small denominational colleges, which did not have the resources or the dynamic quality to compete for students. Nor did they approve of the "irreligious" center that the university was. An even less generous opposition came from the older colleges and universities of the East, led by Eliot of Harvard—opposition that brought to white heat the resentment of the Middle West against the wealthy, aristocratic demigods of New England. In answer to Eliot's attack on free higher education in the state universities—a small-spirited attack arising from the recognition that the state universities would be formidable rivals to the old private universities—Angell said that he could not imagine "anything more hateful, more repugnant to our natural instincts, more calamitous at

once to learning and to the people, more unrepublican, more un-
democratic, more unchristian than a system which should confine the
priceless boon of higher education to the rich."[9] But in spite of opposition, the university made progress and increasingly attracted able
men to its faculty and able students to its classes. The number of
highly trained members of the faculty was steadily increased:
whereas in 1884 Michigan had only six doctors of philosophy in a
total faculty of eighty-eight, more than half the faculty held the
degree twenty-five years later. In 1881 Michigan established an
advanced school for political science. Towards the end of the century
she became a leader in coeducation. After the turn of the year into
the new century, the University of Michigan became the football
leader of the Middle West. A more lasting achievement was President Angell's persuading the Michigan legislature to make an annual
grant to the state university of one twentieth of a mill from the
state's taxes, a figure that was later raised to one tenth of a mill. This
gave the university a stability and flexibility that proved to be
enormous assets in its march to great place in the university world.

Of all American state universities, the University of Wisconsin
developed the idea of service to its state to the highest pitch.[10]
Beginning in the nineteenth century under President John Bascom,
the "Wisconsin Idea" came to its full flowering after 1904 when
Charles R. Van Hise was inaugurated as president. The idea was the
product of many forces of the time, but both the state and the university were ready for it. The university had shared the Land Grant
awards of the federal government in 1862 and 1890, and in the last
decade of the nineteenth century had joined the university movement
by establishing a graduate school of arts and sciences. At the beginning of the new century, the university was already a popular, practical institution, which had successfully withstood the assaults of
denominational colleges and was prepared to meet the needs of the
state as those small and backward colleges could not do. According
to Richard T. Ely, a professor in Madison, the people of Wisconsin

were responsible for the special character of their university, for "they never allowed their university to lose itself in academic unrealities. They knew they wanted something different and new, something responsive to their need, something which they called practical."[11]

The time was, of course, the era of Progressivism, and Robert La Follette the elder was a great power in Wisconsin and the nation. The Progressive Movement proposed to make democracy work, to save the people from the greedy vested interests of wealth and the impure politics of the country. It was, in Wisconsin, a kind of early New Deal, not a little touched with moral righteousness. Van Hise translated all the ferment of the time into a program of service, and he made the concerns of the state and the university so identical that Wisconsin came to be called "the University State." Perhaps most important was the service that the university by its research performed for the agriculture of the state. "The cow," said a friend of the university, "is one of the many by-products of higher education in Wisconsin. For the university saved the dairy industry and brought it to a high state of efficiency."[12] The university provided experts for all aspects of agriculture in Wisconsin and gradually won the affection and loyalty of its farmers. But it was also the home of experts in many other fields, such as forests and utilities, banks and railroads, and especially in government as La Follette put the university economists and political scientists to work upon his legislative program. Yet there was more to be done. Because the university was for the people—and to make democracy work at its best the people had to be educated—the university developed the first and most elaborate program of extension work. This involved making the resources of the university available throughout the state by supplying university courses, lectures, and library services. These admirable arrangements endeared the university to the people and, no doubt, enlarged and made easier the passage of the university budgets. It also made more palatable La Follette's refusal to accept "tainted money" from the foundations for university purposes. In 1908 President Eliot, with as much reason as rashness, could call the University of Wisconsin the leading state university.

The University of Wisconsin had brought to its highest development the idea that the primary function of the university was to be of service to the state. This ideal of immediate and practical usefulness was peculiarly suited to the utilitarian and pragmatic temper of the country, and many other universities adopted it. Though not the purest, or perhaps the highest, conception of the function of a university, the ideal has much validity for tax-supported institutions and has become an article in the American creed.

In a later time, as we shall see, the nation was to lay heavy demands upon the universities of the country for defense, health, and economic betterment. The universities sometimes do become too fastidious in the defense of their independence, but here it seems wise to point out the danger that the university will become regarded, and not only in the popular mind, as only a service station. We must remind ourselves that the freedom of the universities to search for truth is even more important than the immediate services they can perform for society, that learning is often most useful when it is not directed towards immediate utility.

If there were world enough and time, it would be instructive and pleasant to discuss other American universities during the first two decades of the twentieth century—such strong or advancing universities as Columbia and Minnesota, or others, like Clark and Stanford, that suffered disastrous setbacks during this time and would be forced to wait for many years for recovery. But in the main, the major developments of American universities before the First World War are illustrated in the six I have discussed at length.

Columbia, under Barnard, Burgess, Low, and Butler, would illustrate the same points that Harvard exhibited but perhaps in even greater complexity—it was in fact the most completely organized university in the country during the first two decades, possibly the best known internationally of our universities, and the sponsor of the greatest number of learned serial publications, the number reaching thirty-five in 1904.[13] And Minnesota and Illinois would repeat to a large extent the story of progress towards the university idea that we have seen in Michigan and Wisconsin. Perhaps it is enough to say that, by the time the United States entered the First World War, the leading institutions of higher education were moving steadily towards the conception of a university as each interpreted that idea.

In 1900 the universities had banded themselves into the Association of American Universities, and a similar association was formed by the Land Grant Colleges. In his volume *Great American Universities,* published in 1910, E. E. Slosson undertook to appraise the university situation in America and discussed at length the fourteen that he considered the leading ones. Of these, nine were endowed or private institutions: Harvard, Columbia, Chicago, Yale, Cornell, Princeton, Pennsylvania, Stanford, and Johns Hopkins. The case of Cornell was of course ambiguous. Five universities were state-supported: Michigan, Wisconsin, Minnesota, Illinois, and California. Slosson disclaimed any validity in his order of naming the universities, but it is significant that all the fourteen institutions he discussed still maintain their eminent standing fifty-four years later. The various disciplines had well before 1910 formed professional associations, and during the second decade larger groups were established, such as the American Council of Learned Societies in 1919. The professor had become a specialist primarily interested in the advancement of knowledge, and his ties and loyalties had shifted in large part from the college or university he served to his discipline and his fellow workers in that discipline throughout the country. It was the age of organization and professionalism, and in 1915 the Association of University Professors was formed to protect the interests of the individual teacher against unfair treatment by the colleges or universities.

As the century advanced, the university idea grew, and its progress may fairly be measured by the numbers of students enrolled in graduate work. In 1900 the country over, there were 5,668, and this number had passed 6,000 by 1910; by 1930 there were 47,225; and by 1950, with a greater increase still to come in the second half of the century, 233,786. For their significance during the period we are considering, Slosson's figures relating to students in the country's graduate schools are instructive.[14] In 1909, as the universities hovered around 5,000 each in total enrollment, the leading graduate schools registered the following numbers: Columbia, 797; Chicago, 441; Harvard, 423; California, 414; Pennsylvania, 407; Yale, 396; Wisconsin, 250; Hopkins, 178; Stanford, 84. From these small beginnings, where the universities often were little more than colleges and the colleges themselves had to spend much time in preparatory work, have risen our great graduate schools and research centers of today. A further significant fact emerges from Slosson's volume: no university in the South was included in the list of leading universities, and there was no discussion of the large universities closely associated with cities, such as Boston University, New York University, or the University of Cincinnati. These institutions, sometimes supported by their communities but frequently independent or denominational in origin, were usually intimately associated with their regions and served the needs of the neighborhood with programs in commerce, business, and technological studies. They were collegiate in character, and their standards were generally not as high as those of the neighboring universities. In time, however, a number of these municipal universities broadened and liberalized their curriculums, improved their standards, and developed graduate and professional programs of quality. For example, Boston University improved its special interests in divinity and psychology; New York University became very strong in law and the history of art, Syracuse in political science, and Rochester in medicine and music; and Cincinnati became eminent in the classics and archaeology. These were notable achievements. Other municipal institutions that were weak in 1910 were later to become universities of consequence—for example, Buffalo, Denver, and St. Louis, later to be called Washington University.

The development of professional schools as essential parts of the university idea is not uniquely American, but the growth took on many characteristic and native features in the nineteenth and twentieth centuries. First of all, it must be repeatedly stressed that the professional schools illustrate in an emphatic way the tendency of this country to compel its educational institutions into its service, though indeed the universities were not reluctant to be so employed. Indeed, the country's colleges had always been somewhat engaged in preparing young men to enter the older professions, though they had long insisted that the classical curriculum of the eighteenth and nineteenth centuries was adequate for these needs. But this was demonstrably no longer true when the industrial and scientific movements got under way in the nineteenth century. Harvard and Yale both saw the need for establishing scientific schools in the 1850s, but were careful not to let these new ventures infect the old and purer channels of education. The Land Grant Act of 1862 plainly showed the thinking of the country; and schools of agriculture, industrial and mechanical sciences, and technology were established in many states, most successfully as schools in already operating universities. The older professions, divinity, medicine, and law, abandoning the early practices of apprenticeship and proprietary institutions, had already become established as schools. But they were followed at no very great distance by schools for engineers, teachers, business administrators, foresters, journalists, veterinarians, librarians, nurses, social workers, and dietitians, to name a few. It could be fairly said that the distinction had been forgotten between the professions that required learning and those that were more practical and could perhaps be mastered by apprenticeship, observation, and practice. In the egalitarian climate of the United States, all vocations were to be made equal, and if possible all were to be equally respectable.

In the first two decades of the twentieth century, the typical university consisted of a core that was the faculty of arts and sciences serving both the college and the graduate school—which was itself professional in great part—surrounded by a loosely affiliated group of inferior professional schools. In its organization Columbia was the most highly developed. The university had associated Union Theological Seminary with itself as a school of divinity, and the College of Physicians and Surgeons as a medical school. It had developed professional schools in law, mining, journalism, architecture, and teacher education, among other activities, and many of these schools were in the first rank in their kind. As the number and variety of new professional schools grew, one principle could be generally observed in their development over the country: the universities established such schools in answer to the local demand. Thus Cornell and Wisconsin developed schools of agriculture that became internationally famous; California naturally was especially forward in mining, Pennsylvania in business, and Columbia in journalism.

In general the quality of the professional schools, even in the older professions, was poor. Students were often admitted after two years of college, sometimes directly from high school, and the demands of the curriculum were frequently easy and practical. The conception of the study of medicine as deeply rooted in the biological learning and research of the university, or of law as closely connected with the social sciences, was still far in the future. Antiquated methods of instruction—the descriptive textbook, recitation, and lecture—left the student to discover what he could of the theory, often without the benefit of empirical practice.

In 1910, however, an event occurred that galvanized professional training into drastic reform and improvement. This was Abraham Flexner's study of medical education, sponsored by the Carnegie Foundation for the Advancement of Teaching.[15] Flexner found that, in spite of good medical education being given at a few institutions such as Johns Hopkins and Harvard, there were more than a hundred schools that had low academic standards and altogether inadequate equipment. With the publication of Flexner's report, a number of these schools went out of existence, and a few years later only eighty-five much improved medical schools were left. The revolution Flexner brought about in medical education had a far-reaching effect. The American Medical Association had worked closely with Flexner, and now other professional associations began to work with the universities for reform in their fields. By the end of the second decade of the twentieth century, excellent beginnings had been made in many professions and institutions; but the fuller and more satisfactory progress lay several decades ahead, when ampler financial support and better understanding were to lift most of the professional schools to university stature in research and teaching.

Some of the good beginnings of the earlier time, however, deserve recording, especially in the older professions. In divinity the leaders were Yale, Chicago, and Columbia (counting the Union Theological Seminary); in medicine Harvard, Johns Hopkins, Pennsylvania, and Columbia were strong; in law Harvard, Yale, Columbia, and Michigan were most highly regarded; in education Columbia, Chicago, and Michigan were outstanding. Special interests were scattered among the universities over the country. Engineering, for example, in the first decade of the century was probably strongest at Rensselaer Polytechnic Institute, with Cornell, Michigan, and Massachusetts Institute of Technology following.

By the close of the First World War, then, the major ground plans of the universities had been drawn. If service was the primary object of these institutions, and the public was too much inclined to regard them as service stations, the spirit of research and the desire to advance knowledge were nevertheless present. For the encouragement of research, as well as for administrative convenience, the faculties had become completely departmentalized. Very soon after the war new and larger scholarly organizations, dedicated to the furtherance of research in the humanities and the social sciences, were to make their appearance, the American Council of Learned Societies in 1919 and the Social Science Research Council in 1923. Still other aids to the universities for research and teaching were supplied by the great philanthropic organizations, the Carnegie and Rockefeller foundations, both products of the twentieth century. As a sign of coming maturity in learning, the universities of America had begun to produce their own scholars and scientists. The foundations for university development in the future were well and truly laid, though this country was not yet equal partners with Europe in the great enterprise of learning. It was apparent also that our universities and colleges were deeply committed to the service of our scientific, industrial, democratic society. The major lacks were financial support for such ambitious enterprises, and public understanding of the true functions and values of the universities.

CHAPTER IV | HIGHER EDUCATION
BETWEEN TWO WORLD WARS

The two decades between the First and Second World Wars exhibit American society in a standard manic-depressive state. In the twenties the mood of the country gradually became one of high and unhealthy exhilaration; in the thirties the mood was one of profound depression. The earlier decade was at first a period of reaction from the high-pitched emotions engendered by the war and the League of Nations, a reaction that resulted in complete moral slackness and abandonment of responsibility. But within a few years the temper of the country had changed to one of feverish excitement. It was the age of the flapper and the youthful literature of F. Scott Fitzgerald, of Edna St. Vincent Millay and the *carpe diem* philosophy. It became the decade of the bootlegger, the speakeasy, and the speculator, of political corruption and gang murders.

In the colleges of the country this mood was translated into the enormous development of spectator athletics, with hip flasks and raccoon coats in crowded stadiums. Perhaps the developments in football best expressed the temper of the colleges, as the public crowded the bowls and filled the coffers. The great stadiums had been built before the war, and now week after week they were filled with noisy and half-tipsy collegians, hearty alumni and gambling townsmen. The game itself had become more interesting and less brutal as the forward pass replaced the flying wedge. The tramp athlete had been partly eliminated, but sharp practices were still rampant. In this climate the large colleges of the East enjoyed their last fling as football powers in the nation, for it became increasingly apparent that the future would be in the hands of the larger institutions of the Midwest. It was also apparent, as the Praying Colonels of Center College defeated Harvard and Iowa defeated Yale, that any college willing to pay the price could be a national champion. It was also clear that the great Saturday spectacles had little to do with the classroom save to ameliorate the tedium of the large, unrelieved, impersonal lectures. The excoriating report of the Carnegie Foundation on the athletic situation in 1929 left few institutions with a clean bill of health. But the public continued to measure the worth of a college by its athletic successes and to believe, with some reason, that the colleges were essentially country clubs where social gaiety often exploded into an orgy.

The great depression that began in 1929 and merged into the Second World War was one of the most disastrous periods in the country's history. At the beginning of the economic collapse, the mood of the country plunged from uncertainty to despair as all the seemingly solid institutions of society began to show their inadequacy to meet the nation's material and spiritual distress. Despair led to cynicism and to questioning of the deepest loyalties. It was an age of revolt and the seizing of desperate remedies—of civil war in Spain, of the triumph of fascism and Nazism abroad, of defection and treachery, of hunger and suffering at home. In the colleges, where many young people had been driven by the lack of jobs, the winds of opinion buffeted the students sorely and made them call many things into question, especially Wall Street and big business, favorites of the twenties. The revolts and the questionings probably did not go very deep, and the effects certainly were not permanent, as the war years later showed; but events did rouse the social consciences of the students, sharpened their political awareness, and made them more serious and concerned. They were to be seen in picket lines or organizing leftist activities and labor unions. A very few of them became Communists. To many students the most annoying aspect of college life was the careful neutrality of their professors. Some of the professors themselves, however, were often deeply involved in the noises and hoarse disputes of that distressing time.

In the twenties the universities of the country had reached a temporary pause in their development and were busy consolidating their gains and tightening their organizations, though all the while continuing to grow in size and activity. To the acute distress of many fiercely loyal college alumni, the university, with its now firmly established graduate and professional schools, absorbed more and more of the resources and the interest of the educational world and presented to the public a clearer and simpler reason for their support. In spite of the overshadowing universities, however, there occurred in the twenties and continued into the thirties a strong reassertion of collegiate values. In the *Atlantic Monthly* for November 1921, the historian Wilbur Cortez Abbott wrote an article called "The Guild of the Students." Here he asserted that the American college was a great deal more than the buildings, the faculty, and the curriculum. It was an educational institution that the undergraduate had made for himself, and it consisted of fraternities and clubs, teams and groups engaged in various activities. It had laws and rewards of its own, and these were rigorously applied. The way of life devised by the collegians of the twenties had little to do with the formal purposes of the college, but served admirably as preliminary training for the rough competitive world the students would enter after graduation. The collegiate world that Canby had seen at the beginning of the century was still flourishing.

THE COLLEGES

The first thing to notice about the colleges of this time is their large increase in enrollment. In 1919–20 there were approximately 600,000 students enrolled in the country's colleges; ten years later this figure had grown to 1,100,000; by 1939–40 the number had risen to 1,500,000. This growth was much faster than that of the population at large. In 1919–20 only 8.14 percent of young people were in college;

in 1939–40 the percentage was 15.32.[1] Also to be noted is the pervasive tendency at the time, beginning in the East but spreading widely through the country, for the colleges to assume again the duty of educating the student as a whole person—morally, culturally, and socially as well as intellectually. This movement, undoubtedly a reaction to the greater size of the institutions and to the impersonality and remoteness of the prevailing methods of instruction, probably also owed something to the distress of the elders at the manners and morals of the postwar generation. The effort to improve college life took many forms. At Yale, for example, a freshman year common to all students, whatever their future intentions, was established with its own dean and curriculum, its own faculty whose members were to be rewarded for excellent teaching equally with the scholars of the university, its own resident and academic counselors, and its own living quarters. A separate freshman year, however, was not widely adopted, and at Yale it finally foundered upon two hard rocks—the departmental organization that promoted faculty members only for scholarly production, and the programs of advanced placement and standing that made impossible any plan of a common curriculum. But the trend to better counseling and living quarters was later to be extended for the benefit of upperclassmen, as we shall see.

Many new offices began to be established in the colleges: deans of all kinds and functions; chaplains and career consultants; elaborate departments of health, containing a corps of psychiatrists in the wealthier institutions as the years went on; offices that dispensed financial aid to students and managed the National Youth Administration funds when the government had to come to the aid of the students and the colleges in the years of the depression; and finally offices of educational research to advise the colleges in the problems of admissions, scholarships, examinations, and standards. This last development was sometimes a kind of narcissism, but generally it was advantageous for institutions to know what they were doing well and what poorly, and to compare local standards with such national ones as they could obtain. Such expansions were most onerous to those colleges that did not have the finances to support these improvements; but even the wealthier colleges found the arrangements hard to meet, especially if they were aiding the development of their institutions into universities, as was often the case.

The complexities that worried the many college officials were not made easier by the conditions of the time. As we have seen, the universities, modeled on the German idea, cared little for the morals and manners of their students. Only the intellectual aspects of the student's education were important. Then too the colleges of the nineteenth century frequently had not had the financial resources to house and feed their students, though the older colleges sometimes had inadequate dormitory arrangements surviving from an earlier time. Mainly for these reasons, almost every campus in America had allowed an elaborate system of residential fraternities to develop. Students too poor, or those disinclined to join the fraternities, lived in boarding houses or in private homes. Women, both in the women's colleges and in coeducational institutions, usually fared better, since dormitories had to be provided for their care. At Cornell University in the twenties and thirties most of the women were housed and fed in handsome residential units owned and operated by the university; freshmen, too, were housed in a university dormitory. The men students, however, for the greater part lived under little or no supervision in some seventy-five fraternities, some of which were palaces, comparable to the famous eating clubs at Princeton, but others were desperately poor. The conditions of living arrangements at Cornell were typical, I think, of the American college that had grown so large after the First World War.

The older colleges of the East, drawn as they were on the English model, had always assumed the responsibility for the housing and feeding of their students. With less certainty in the twentieth century, they still acknowledged their responsibility for the manners, morality, and the character of their charges. But as new students arrived in ever greater numbers, the living arrangements of these colleges had deteriorated sadly and were now seen to be haphazard and inadequate. Further, the catch-as-catch-can accommodations disclosed to the public the sharp differences between rich and poor students, a difference acutely painful to egalitarian sentiment in the country.

Many colleges began to build dormitories for their students, first usually for freshmen who needed most the care and supervision. The older ideal of the colonial college was emphatically reasserted in the late twenties and early thirties when Harvard and Yale, alarmed by the size of their undergraduate schools and the lack of faculty supervision for the students, were enabled by the generosity of Edward S. Harkness to construct their residential houses and colleges. Each of these units had a master and a corps of faculty fellows, some of them resident, and many of them with offices in the unit. Each unit, also, had its dining hall, its library, its program of athletics and activities, language clubs and dramatic or singing groups. The units were small in order to recapture the advantages of the earlier small college, and ideally all students beyond the freshman year could be accommodated. Distinctions between the rich and poor students were to be eliminated by scholarships and jobs that were more attractive than waiting on table. But no formal educational functions were given to the residential units at first, and only lately have a few such responsibilities been allotted them. In the meanwhile, the living conditions of the students at Yale and Harvard were enormously improved, and so were the cultural, social, and moral aspects of student life.

In the thirties, however, the plans for the houses and colleges at Yale and Harvard were not widely imitated. This was partly because such a development was very expensive at a time when funds were scarce, but partly, too, because the English idea did not generally appeal to the democratic conception of college life. Other events were happening in America at the same time which were much more native and democratic. Under the pressure of numbers, several states began to expand their systems of public higher education. In Michigan, where the university at Ann Arbor ever since the presidency of Angell had been the head of public education, this expansion took the form of branch institutions such as Michigan State College—institutions that were allowed to attain full status as four-year colleges. The expansion has continued to the present day. In California, which had earlier followed the example of Michigan, the same movement brought about the establishment of the University of California at Los Angeles. This development is also continuing, but here and elsewhere a variant solution has brought about the establishment of junior colleges as feeders, in part, for the central university. The idea was not new; Harper at Chicago had earlier thought the lower college a rational and convenient division of the university. Many of the new junior colleges merely extended the local high school by adding two years of further training, frequently of a vocational nature. In any case, the junior-college movement grew rapidly. In 1920 there were 52 such colleges in the country; in 1930 there were 277; in 1941 there were about 450. No doubt, the years of the depression encouraged the growth of these colleges.

Many of the weaker four-year colleges were in grave peril from the depression and the proliferation of junior colleges, but few of them went out of business. Instead, some of the junior colleges that began with vocational intentions gradually transformed themselves into liberal-arts junior colleges, so great was the prestige of the strong colleges of the arts and sciences. Likewise a number of teachers' colleges, founded on the model of teachers' colleges at Columbia or Chicago, made themselves into complete liberal-arts colleges of good quality. This development could be seen at Albany and Montclair, but it happened elsewhere and is still happening today at an accelerated pace.

The most persistent efforts of the colleges in the two decades following the end of the First World War were devoted to the shaping of a modern curriculum that would recognize the new breadth of knowledge, but would at the same time achieve a satisfactory design and perform a function in the total educational plan. Almost equally important was the related effort to achieve standards of excellence in the face of the ever increasing numbers of students. The new necessity was to bring order out of disorder: to construct a program of studies appropriate to the new age, rational in its direction and sequences, comprehensive enough in its scope to include the new learning, rigorous enough in its demands, and flexible enough to allow the gifted student to develop his full potential. In short, it was now the task of the college to justify its existence, to reassert its integrity, and to assume the intellectual leadership of the nation as it had not done for many years.

By 1920 the results of the elective system were known. Its good effects decidedly outweighed the bad ones. Most important, the system had enabled colleges to become universities by expanding the areas of knowledge to include the natural sciences and later the social sciences and by ordering the whole spectrum of knowledge into convenient departments. Next, the system freed the individual to pursue the studies in which he was most interested and relieved him of the necessity of studying those to which he was hostile. It put a premium upon eagerness and freedom in the act of learning, and this led to higher individual standards. But there were also deficits. Too often the curriculum was utterly without pattern and comprised a great number of short and sometimes superficial courses. The very freedom that the system provided invited the less serious student to dabble in his studies or to devote his time exclusively to studies that were of little worth or not appropriate to his stage of learning. Further, the system virtually wiped out a number of the humanistic parts of the old curriculum, such as the study of Greek and ultimately of Latin, and put a premium upon the immediate and practical, a tendency to which America was perhaps too prone. The balance, then, was struck, and few colleges strongly missed the old common curriculum or wished back the old college of the nineteenth century. The problem was to contain and order the new freedom in all its aspects; and this the colleges began slowly to do in the third and fourth decades of the century.

A preliminary step towards a new arrangement had been taken a good deal earlier. In his inaugural address in 1909, Harvard's new president, A. Lawrence Lowell, spoke out against the elective system for its failure to educate the student properly, either intellectually or socially; and he proposed a system of distribution and concentration in college studies that is the germ of the plan in almost universal use today. Further progress was made in 1910 as many colleges, led by Bryn Mawr, adopted the practice of grouping the subjects of instruction and requiring the student to take work in each group. From these beginnings there gradually developed a common pattern of requiring two courses for the sake of distribution in each of the three large categories, the humanities, the natural sciences, and the social sciences. But the matter was not immediately clear in the 1920s. What were the subjects to be included in each group? And what was to be done with the older learning, specifically Greek and Latin? Greek had gone, but the Latin requirement, both for entrance to college and for the bachelor's degree, was fought for bitterly. In time the matter was compromised. Alternative programs and new degrees, such as the bachelor of philosophy, were invented, requiring no Latin and emphasizing science. The ancient languages were usually grouped with modern foreign languages and a choice was allowed. Imperceptibly, English language and literature took over the task of providing for the literary aspect of the student's education, and in some institutions the classics were partially protected by courses in translation or ancient history as alternatives to work in the languages themselves.

The arrangement of studies into required groups solved, in a fashion and for a while, the problem of distribution and assured the college that the student would have at least a superficial acquaintance with the major areas of learning. But that was only half the problem. Something else was needed to ensure that the student's education would not be a haphazard collection of elementary courses, but would have in it a rational progress to maturity and mastery. Again, earlier in the century there had been gropings towards major and minor concentrations of courses in the student's last two years of college. Indeed, the elective system at its freest had allowed the student to concentrate his studies in a narrow field if he chose to do so. In the twenties, and on into the thirties, the aspect of concentration as a vital part of the student's training received much attention. It was seen that it was not enough for the student's development that in his last years of college he should elect a number of courses in a single subject. Comprehensive examinations in the field of concentration were introduced—a practice that spread to many colleges. To prepare the student for these examinations, tutorial and seminarial instruction was necessary. A further elaboration of the major was the requirement of independent work from the senior, either an essay of considerable length or a limited research project in one of the sciences. The danger here lay in requiring of the student premature research of a graduate nature, and this has not always been avoided. But, on the whole, the movement has been an invigorating and powerful force towards regaining for the college the integrity of its function and confirming its place in the total educational establishment.

The ideas making towards the modern curriculum came from many colleges. Before the First World War, Princeton under Woodrow Wilson had adopted the promising preceptorial plan, and in the twenties and thirties most good colleges adopted honors programs for their better students. Many colleges, large and small, contributed to the honors idea, but none more significantly than Swarthmore. One should also mention the quality of undergraduate work done at the women's colleges, Bryn Mawr, Vassar, Smith, and Wellesley, the admirable progress in independent work done at Reed and the introduction of outside examiners by Wells. Meiklejohn's innovations at

Wisconsin showed that the state universities also were interested in quality and experiment in undergraduate education. His two-year plan at Wisconsin foreshadowed the arrangement later adopted by St. John's College at Annapolis, as students concentrated their attention upon Athens in the first year and contemporary America in the second.[2] A program decidedly American in its size and democracy was established at the University of Minnesota. This was the General College, which was to care for the less competent student.[3] Elsewhere, the colleges were committed to other programs, such as Columbia's plan of combining studies in the last two years of college with work in one of the professional schools; and there was a somewhat similar plan at Chicago that, after a two-year bachelor's degree, combined the major with work for a master's degree in a three-year program.

Honors programs were developed in almost every substantial college in the land, but perhaps the resurgence of the colleges in the third decade of this century, and their drive towards excellence, may be seen best in the program that Frank Aydelotte established at Swarthmore in 1922.[4] This program, modeled on Oxford where Aydelotte had been a Rhodes Scholar, set the honors candidates apart from pass students; it allowed the honors student to concentrate his work in a single field; it provided tutorial and seminarial instruction for him; it required not only comprehensive written examinations and an oral examination conducted in part by examiners from other institutions, but also a thesis exhibiting independent work. The Swarthmore program, much admired, possessed a number of features that deserve comment. The fact that it was modeled on Oxford was significant because it signalled a return, in collegiate education at least, from the German plan to the British. Further, the small seminars and the personal association between the student and his teacher represented a drastic change from the impersonal lecture system which generally prevailed in the colleges, especially those colleges in a university context. Finally, the demand of the Swarthmore program for independent work in the student's papers and thesis emphasized the possibilities for intellectual work of a high quality in the American undergraduate at his best. If there was a flaw in the conception it was that, since the American high schools had not caught up with Winchester and Eton, for a number of students too large a degree of concentration was imposed upon an inadequate base of general knowledge.

Not all colleges were happy with what had been achieved in the reconstruction of the curriculum. The discontent was mainly with the arrangements for distribution in the student's program. The compromise of group requirements did not state clearly what an educated man ought to know. To some, the group-requirement arrangement was a solution of expediency and did not discriminate among subjects, which were all presented as of equal value and as equally appropriate to any stage of the student's learning. The improvement upon the elective system seemed inadequate, and the proliferation of courses in the humanities, the natural sciences, and the social sciences confronted the student with a bewildering array of offerings at a time when he was most inexperienced and least prepared to choose wisely for his future education. In the system of group requirements there was hardly any design or philosophy at all. Further, under the strong tendency towards departmentalization the elementary courses in each subject, which were the ones offered in the group requirements, were usually taught as if the student were going to pursue that subject to his doctor's degree. In short, to many people the curriculum that would take the place of the old integrated curriculum of the nineteenth century had not been found.

The first motion towards a new plan came from Columbia College, a modest beginning that was to lead in time to the movement known as General Education.[5] During the First World War Columbia had devised a course in "war issues" that had proved to be very successful. This course stressed the Western intellectual and spiritual tradition as embodying a large part of what an educated man needed to know and understand. With the aid of his faculty, Dean Herbert Hawkes adapted the course to normal conditions and developed other courses to accompany it in a full program of general education. In the plan there were three sequences, each consisting of two courses in the humanities, in the natural sciences, and in the social sciences. These courses were interdisciplinary rather than departmental, were taught by teachers drawn from all departments, and had the special virtue of giving the student a wider view of knowledge than he could get from the election of courses in single disciplines. The design was imaginative in conception and has continued to operate to the present, except that the natural sciences have abandoned their sequence on the ground that such interdepartmental courses are inadequate to their need for specialization. Here, then, was born the idea of general education; it was to have a long and interesting future as the colleges strove to impose an adequate pattern, and some discrimination, upon the vast body of knowledge confronting the student.

Quite as drastic and bold were the changes in the curriculum that were introduced in the program of the University of Chicago.[6] Unhappy with the state of things in the College in the twenties, and especially with the featureless survey courses of the curriculum, Chicago undertook to reform liberal education from the ground up. As at Columbia, a prime purpose was to avoid the fragmentation of learning and to achieve an integration in the studies of the student's early years. The greatest novelty was the division of the College into a lower and an upper unit. The lower college, four years in length, was to allow students who had finished two years of high school to come to Chicago as college students and to take their bachelor's degrees at an age when, in the usual college procedure, they would only have completed their sophomore year. The same program of courses was prescribed for all students, with no attendance requirement. The faculty was organized into four major areas or divisions: the biological sciences, the physical sciences, the social sciences, and the humanities. When the student had passed the prescribed general course in each of these areas, he was qualified to enter as a majoring student in one of the four divisions, and in three additional years he could obtain his master's degree. As in the honors program at Swarthmore, the examining arrangements were dissociated from the instructional ones; but at Chicago a special examining organization was maintained as a part of the institution. One feature, taken from Columbia,[7] was the emphasis Chicago placed upon "Great Books" in its program; and encouraged by President Hutchins in the thirties, the plan was invested with a metaphysical philosophy. The general plan was influential in the country and still persists at Chicago in the main, but in 1960 the admission of students to college before they had finished high school was largely abandoned.

The changes at Chicago were bold, but it was difficult to impose a new conception in all its functioning reality upon a famous, complex institution that already was deep in its university development. Therefore, when the old conventional college of St. John's at Annapolis became bankrupt and was about to suspend activity, Hutchins of Chicago saw an opportunity to set up a thoroughgoing model of his idea of what a liberal education should be. With the strong support of Chicago, St. John's was taken over and a novel curriculum was installed. This curriculum, devoted to "the single-minded pursuit of the intellectual virtues," was an attempt to reinvoke something comparable to the medieval trivium and quadrivium; and the saints of the venture were Aristotle and Thomas Aquinas. The ordering principle, however, was to be not religion but metaphysics—a conception more acceptable to the modern mind. The materials for study were the great books of human history, taught in seminars and colloquia and employing Socratic discussion at every opportunity, as the studies moved chronologically from Greece and Rome to the present. Stringfellow Barr and Scott Buchanan went from Chicago to put the program into operation, as Hutchins and Adler at Chicago, Mark Van Doren at Columbia, and traditional humanists elsewhere who were unhappy with higher education in America watched with sympathy.

Columbia and Chicago, with an experimental model in St. John's, were the leaders in these early ventures that strove to provide a means of ameliorating the fragmentation of learning caused by the elective system and specialization. The movement called General Education, though differing in many details from institution to institution, was to enjoy a wide future development after the end of the Second World War. Its high point at this later time was reached in Harvard's well-known report of 1945, *General Education in a Free Society,* of which more will be said in a later chapter. The tendency of general education to restore a prescribed curriculum made up of interdisciplinary courses has been strongly challenged by the great varieties of ability and achievement among students and by the reluctance of many departments to cooperate in interdisciplinary ventures. Programs of general education at Columbia, Harvard, and Yale are now undergoing serious reappraisals; the program at Harvard does not rely upon interdepartmental courses and may for that reason have a less difficult adjustment to make.

But even in the 1930s, when the traditional humanists in education were trying to establish a curriculum to replace the classical one, there was a strong countermovement. The Progressive Movement, which earlier had a strong effect upon secondary education, now invaded collegiate education in the hard time of the great depression. The prophet of this movement was of course John Dewey, whose *Democracy and Education,* published in 1916, provided the implementing doctrine. In contrast to prescribed curriculums, Dewey spoke for an educational program adapted to the needs and interests of the individual student; this student-centered education should be both functional and contemporary and should represent the total active life of the participant. The student, moreover, should take charge of his own education, selecting his problems and areas of interest and pursuing them in library, laboratory, studio, workshop, or the world of business and affairs beyond the college walls. Education and experience were one and the same thing, and the success of the student could be measured by his adjustment to life—life contemporary and full of practical problems that were not primarily intellectual, perhaps, but were those that engaged the whole personality and character. Dewey's tenets, which had earlier been extremely influential in secondary education through the teachers' colleges, thus entered higher education.

The impact of Dewey's thinking resulted in the founding of a number of so-called progressive colleges and the making over of some traditional ones. Antioch with its combination of work and study— life on the campus alternating with a job in business or industry— began its program as early as 1921. But the full wave of such experimental colleges did not come until a decade later, when the times were more propitious. In rapid succession in the early thirties, Black Mountain College, Bennington, and Sarah Lawrence were established, and older institutions such as Goddard and St. Stephen's (Bard) were reconstructed on progressive principles. Though they did not adopt completely the Dewey line of thought, as did the experimental colleges, most American colleges and universities were affected by it. The progressive colleges introduced a host of new subjects to the course of study, though often these were only adaptations of old materials under new names—communications, physical health, mental health, humanities, social and civic relations, consumer training, and family relations. Psychology, instead of philosophy that had served as a center for the humanists, provided the pervading spirit of the new colleges. In the older institutions Dewey's thought, aided by the hard conditions of the depression, emphasized the social sciences—economics, government, and sociology—which were pertinent to contemporary conditions and had a vigorous development at this time. As a side effect, many colleges made an effort to elevate such extracurricular activities as drama, music, journalism, and debating to the position of respectable subjects for study, in order to engage the interest of the student which, Dewey argued, was the best beginning for an active education. By all these developments higher education and society were brought closer together, and this result would have met Dewey's complete approval. At its best, the effect of his thought was to revitalize collegiate education; at its worst

—and there were bad effects—it diluted the intellectual content and standards of the educational enterprise.

The battle of ideas that stirred the interest of higher education in the 1930s was between the progressive and the conservative positions, and each had its able spokesman, John Dewey for the progressive and Robert Hutchins for the conservative. The philosophy of pragmatism was a native American product, and in the days of the depression was generally in possession of the field. As it applied to education, Dewey's philosophy stressed the empirical and experimental and objected to the notion that theory should be the province of the college and that practice should be assigned to the technical schools and life itself. Ideas and concepts, he thought, could not be effectively taught without experiment, experience, and practice. Concepts themselves were not reality, but only ways of knowing reality. He looked upon logic as a tool and cautioned against too much faith in rationalism as a goal of learning. Moreover, he thought that liberal education should be concerned with moral as well as intellectual values, and that the most liberal studies in any age were those which were devoted to the problems of that age. Education must be constantly changing to meet the necessities of the time and place. Therefore, in America democracy, liberalism, and experiment should comprise the core and method of education. He favored the study of the sciences and the social sciences and thought it was impossible to maintain any distinction between liberal and utilitarian studies.

Against this pervasive, popular theory, Hutchins rose to speak for the conservative position.[8] He found higher education in this country in a wretched state of disorder, and with excoriating wit he blasted American colleges—the somnolent ones, the finishing-school ones, the ones devoted to the cult of success, the socially centered ones, the intensely secular ones and the athletic ones. He found education debased by empiricism, misled by the notion of progress in intellectual matters and by vocationalism and the ideal of student adjustment. The purpose of education, he thought, should be to cultivate the intellect; intellectual excellence should be its exclusive goal, which could best be gained by the study of the wisdom of the ages, preserved in great books. Such study would provide theoretical perspective. In Hutchins' thinking, metaphysics was the heart of the curriculum and lent order and stability to the quest for the intellectual virtues.

The battle was thus joined. Hutchins' attack was salutary for higher education and compelled a good deal of self-inspection in the universities. But it was a revolt rather than a revolution. The naturalistic, utilitarian temper of the country and its tendency towards the democratization of men and ideas were too strong to be much changed. It was soon said that Hutchins' ideas were out of tune with the country and the times, that his conception of education looked backward rather than forward, and that it was touched with authoritarianism. Moreover, it turned away from modern subjects—from the natural and social sciences—and tended to treat knowledge as a fixed matter, settled centuries ago and not subject to change.[9]

These, then, were the alarms and excursions of collegiate education between the two world wars. It should be added that the conventional colleges were not unaffected by the progressive and conservative doctrines and experiments. Most of the colleges were eclectic in their practices and added innovations in matter and method to their programs; notably there was a greater interest in the social sciences, as befitted the time. They also continued to refine and tighten their standard and honors programs. No lasting solution of the problem of the curriculum was found, though valiant efforts to synthesize the curriculum, successful for a time, were made at Columbia, Chicago, St. John's, and elsewhere. A strong movement rose in some Eastern colleges, with the purpose of reassuming the obligation of educating the whole man. In these decades the colleges, though overshadowed by the universities, reasserted their function and their integrity; and once again, as the ideational battle continued its noisy encounter, the old and the new confronted each other, and the English model of the college strove for recognition against the German conception of the university. A truce in the verbal battle was called on December 7, 1941, as once again war began to empty the campuses of their usual students and soldiers of many kinds and ages came to take their places.

THE UNIVERSITIES: GRADUATE AND PROFESSIONAL SCHOOLS

While the colleges were struggling to regain their sense of direction in the two decades following the end of the First World War, the graduate and professional schools were, less visibly, making substantial progress in stability, numbers of students, resources, policy, and standards. At the beginning of the period we are considering, the universities seemed to have reached a plateau, a pausing place where they could consider their past progress, regroup their forces, and plan their future. The first excitement of the university movement was somewhat abated. The elective system had done its work in shattering the old curriculum, thereby allowing the natural and social sciences to take their full places in the studies of the university—indeed, in making the development of the university possible. The effects were far-reaching. The new studies freed the universities from denominational control where that was necessary, opened minds to new possibilities in thought, and directed the attention of the academic world to the secular and the contemporary.

By 1920 the universities had reached a stage of maturity. The organization as a whole had become compact and was certainly more orderly. The major departmental lines had been marked out, and within the department the hierarchy had been established, from the full professor at the top to the lowest instructor. The complex organization that was now the university was usually managed by a large bureaucracy presided over by a secular president who naturally could not maintain his scholarship in his busy office. He in turn was responsible to a board of trustees, largely made up of alumni lawyers and businessmen. The policy of the universities had been set as service to the community and the nation—an adaptation of the extremely successful Wisconsin idea to new times and different conditions—and this ideal invariably meant an unreserved commitment to democracy.

In this mood and climate the universities grew and prospered. As we have seen, the student population of the institutions almost tripled between 1920 and 1940, most of the increase being in the colleges but the graduate and professional schools growing in numbers proportionately. In these years the state universities began their growth towards the gigantic institutions that they have now become. The financial resources of the universities grew even faster than the numbers of students. In 1920 the total endowment of higher education was approximately $570 million; by 1940 that figure had become one billion, 765 million. The decade of the twenties especially was a time of large benefactions, and the endowments of the universities rose sharply. The growth in income was proportionately greater too, as the states by vastly increased appropriations showed their faith in higher education.[10] It needs to be added, however, that the costs of higher education grew even faster, and the period of the depression was a time of financial distress and anxiety in almost every university.

Nevertheless, on the university scene development and change took place in many quarters. Institutions that for one reason or another had been delayed in their full development as universities now began to take their positions as leaders. On the East coast this could nowhere better be seen than at Yale, which had valued and clung to the college ideal too long. The drastic reform of the structure of the university in 1919 prepared the way, and under James Rowland Angell, the first president since colonial days who was not a graduate of Yale College, the institution began its hard climb to a larger eminence as a university. In a few years the graduate and professional schools became first-rate, each in its kind, and the emotional loyalty of the alumni to the college was gradually transformed into pride in the university. A comparable movement took place in the South as that region began to recover slowly from its poverty. The University of North Carolina profited from the intense loyalty the state felt for its own institution, and substantial departments and divisions of service to the state and the nation could be seen in the quality of the research and teaching in rural sociology. The transformation of Trinity College in the same state into Duke University, with an increasingly large income from a private endowment, promised well for the future. A portion of this promise was soon made good by the rising quality of the Duke Medical School. Comparable progress was made by Vanderbilt, Emory, and Tulane, each institution making a special advance in one field or another, as both Vanderbilt and Emory did in medicine.[11] Still, when the Second World War began, it could not yet be said that the South had achieved a university of the first rank, comparable to the great ones of the North and West; but the promise was great and the plans for the future were sound.

Most of the institutions mentioned above are, of course, private universities. Perhaps a more significant development for the future lay in the growth between the two world wars of the great state universities of the Midwest and the West. In the Midwest institutions long established, but earlier little more than colleges, began to assume true university stature, with the full panoply of graduate work of high quality and substantial professional schools. Such institutions come to mind as Minnesota, Iowa, Missouri, and Kansas.[12] Minnesota, indeed, represented a strong continuation of progress begun earlier, but the others named above were in effect almost new developments as universities. Other state universities in the area that had developed the university idea earlier, such as Michigan and Indiana, grew in numbers and quality and matched the eminence of Wisconsin. In the Far West the tremendous climb to greatness of the University of California at Berkeley, not only in size but in quality, began in these two decades and prepared for the position which that university was to achieve after the Second World War. The impressive rise of the State University of Washington and the University of California at Los

Angeles, and the resurgence of Stanford as a university, began in these years, but was delayed in fullness until after the war.[13]

At this point, a few very general observations on the progress of American universities in the twenties and thirties may be pertinent. Without exception they were secular institutions, strongly oriented towards the ideal of immediate service to the state and nation, but also committed to the conception of a basic but distant notion of service to mankind through research and the advancement of knowledge. As the older universities grew in size and wealth, new ones rose to challenge their pre-eminence; but the older institutions often showed a remarkable ability to revitalize and reform themselves. The fourteen universities that Slosson had thought the country's greatest in the first decade of the century still held their places. As had frequently been true in the history of American higher education, the progress of a university was usually owing to the vision and energy of a great president. Leadership was still the most important asset in a university—and this in spite of the fact that the university of the time matched its enormous growth in size by an equal growth in complexity and was in danger of becoming an intricate machine of many delicate and almost autonomous parts.

The tightly organized university of these years corresponded surely to the industrialized society that supported it. Both had expanded in size and grown in complexity. Corporate bureaucracies had developed as a means of governing universities as well as large industrial plants. The president who headed the university was a different creature from the clergyman president of the nineteenth century or his pioneering successor. He was now a man of affairs, chosen by a board of trustees who were themselves captains of industry and managers of business, and he was responsible to an alumni body of the same occupations and beliefs. The president himself was usually not a businessman, but the tasks he was expected to perform were largely those of such a person. He was a man of affairs; he was skilled in finances and public relations; he could raise money and make soul-stirring speeches. At home he was the only person who could compromise differences and reconcile warring forces; abroad he was a showman, and some said a liar and a hypocrite. Hopefully, he was a national figure, a spokesman for education. Often his most difficult task during these stormy years was to explain a politically unorthodox faculty to a conservative board of trustees and a passionately conservative alumni body. An almost equally difficult task was to justify the actions and opinions of the board to a faculty keenly aware of its hard-won freedoms. As the head of a corporate bureaucracy, the president was usually consumed by immediate organizational detail and seldom was fully intimate with the developing educational policy of his institution.

To perform the innumerable tasks of the universities, a huge body of administrators was created. In 1933 it was estimated that there was a median figure of 30.5 administrators for each institution.[14] Nor was the president in many instances able to be closely acquainted with the members of his faculty, and he was even more removed from the students. A provost or a vice-president assumed his home duties with the faculty, and the dean became the image and legendary figure to the student that the nineteenth-century college president had been.[15] It took a very dynamic president indeed to transcend his institution and the conditions of the time and become a figure comparable in importance to the pioneers—Gilman, Eliot, White, and Harper—in the history of education. Very few such giants emerged. Only the president could give direction and purpose to the university; but the university of the twenties and thirties demanded other and lesser qualities as well as leadership—patience, perseverance, an ability to compromise, and some said cunning as well.

The strong trend of the country at large towards secularism, under the impact of science, technology, and industrialism in the late nineteenth century, continued into the twentieth and, as we have seen, made the management and control of the universities secular as well.

In 1860 clergymen made up 30 percent of the members of the boards of trustees in private institutions. This figure had dropped to 7 percent by 1930.[16] The boards of the twentieth century were likely to be made up of industrialists, lawyers, and other men of affairs, and in the state universities there was often a forceful group of politicians. The competence of such lay boards, and often their sympathies, was well outside the purposes and interests of the university, and this was frequently the cause of friction with the faculty, which was becoming increasingly aware of its freedom and status. The trustees were usually elected, in part or as a whole, from the alumni body of the institution. So the board was usually composed of graduates of the university's college, an arrangement that had advantages as well as disadvantages. The loyalty of the alumni was cultivated and paid off handsomely in financial returns; but this also meant that they had the rights of stockholders in the enterprise and frequently exercised their right to question and interfere. Often the alumni were nostalgic obstructors of the progress of the institution; but often, too, only the generous financial support of the alumni saved the universities in times of crisis. It was clearly up to the colleges to see that their graduates became better educated, and especially that they were made sympathetic to the purposes of the modern university.

The professors were of course the heart of the university. They were imbued with a professional spirit. By this time they were being educated at home in the rigid system of the Ph.D. American society required skilled specialists, and they were trained to be such in the scientific manner. Moreover, the continental conception of higher education was reinforced in this country by a new wave of immigrants fleeing from Nazism, fascism, and communism, much to the enrichment of learning here. The new member of the faculty brought his credo with him—*Lehrfreiheit*, freedom of inquiry and freedom to teach. He fitted easily into the rigid departmental structure of the university, and within the department he took his place in the hierarchy. The faculty member, foreign or native, understood the conditions of his appointment and his promotion—he must engage in research and publish his results. His loyalty was not given to the institution he served, or perhaps even to his department, but rather to his profession and to colleagues in the same discipline all over the world. He was not yet the itinerant professor he was to become after the Second World War, but like his president he was a man of affairs and might be called to Washington to advise or take part in the affairs of the Roosevelt administration. He was a person of consequence in the life of the nation as he had not been before.

As the faculty member became more and more professionalized, it is hardly surprising to find that he had created the instruments for his self-expression, his security, and his freedom. As early as the beginning of the twentieth century he had founded professional societies, such as the American Historical Society, for the exchange of professional ideas, and established learned periodicals to keep his discipline alive to contemporary research and thinking. After the turn of the century he began to win sabbatical and pension rights[17] and tenure; and in 1915 an institution was created to safeguard the conditions and freedom of his profession—the American Association of University Professors. The freedom of the professor in the matter of opinion and expression had taken a turn in keeping with the age. In the nineteenth century the matter most questioned was the professor's religious orthodoxy. But soon, in the secularized and business age of the nation, he was most often challenged for his dangerous economics when he expressed himself upon such topics as labor unions, the distribution of wealth, and the management of money. In the heated atmosphere of the thirties, however, the field of challenge was most often politics as the liberal or sometimes radical professor voiced his views, to the horror of a conservative board of trustees. In the American Association of University Professors the academic man found a stout defender of his freedom to speak and to rest secure in his tenure of office and in the conditions in which he worked.[18]

An issue of increasing concern to the American Association of University Professors was the academic salary scale. The professor of the nineteenth century was fortunate to make a salary of $2,500 at the height of his career. Late in the century in a few places, such as Chicago and Harvard, he might have a salary of $4,000, but in many poor colleges his salary was reckoned in hundreds rather than thousands. Some improvement occurred early in the twentieth century, but progress was painfully slow and salaries were always subject to cuts in times of crisis.[19] Perhaps the close association between the teacher and the clergyman did encourage the nineteenth-century professor to forgo a proper financial reward for his labor; but it was surely unkind of President Eliot in his inaugural address in 1869 to make a national virtue of the condition: "The poverty of scholars is of inestimable worth in this money-getting nation. It maintains the true standards of virtue and honor." By 1908 Eliot had learned nothing: "The profession can never be properly recruited by holding out pecuniary inducements." One can only paraphrase Wordsworth: "Eliot! thou shouldst be living at this hour." Even in the third decade of the present century *The Nation* and *The New Republic* applauded the idea of low salaries for professors, as incitements to virtue.[20] In the nineteen-thirties, when in strong institutions professors' salaries were rarely as much as $7,500 and instructors' were $1,800, both were sometimes cut by a quarter or a half, and in those distressing times the Association could do little to aid. But it was there to speak for the profession, and in time by constant pressure it was able to improve the salaries of the profession appreciably. The Association in many ways was the professor's union.

A few words must be said about the graduate training required of the professor at this time. The Ph.D. has often been called the professor's union card, and by 1930 it was becoming necessary for a teacher in a college or a university to have the doctor's degree if he wished to rise to the top of the profession. From the small award of three Ph.D.s by Yale in 1861, the granting of the degree spread rapidly. In 1930, at 74 institutions 2,024 Ph.D.s were awarded, and in that same year 47,255 students were enrolled in the country's graduate schools.[21] These figures emphasize the fact that the United States was producing its own scholars and teachers and no longer depended upon the German universities. A second fact is that the pattern of training given for the doctor's degree had not altered, but remained set to the German model. It was a training profoundly influenced by the scientific revolution and was directed towards research and the advancement of knowledge. It paid little heed to the fact that 90 percent of the new doctors of philosophy would enter the teaching profession, that once their dissertations were accepted, most of them would never undertake further research. But in spite of sharp criticism, early and late, the Ph.D. continues to flourish, and universities and colleges are often rated by the number of Ph.D.s they can count on their faculties.

The immediately noticeable fact concerning the advanced schools for training in the major professions during the two decades after the First World War is that at their best they had joined their universities in full form and spirit—when, that is, they had become great centers of research in their respective fields while continuing to prepare young men and women to become active practitioners in a profession. Moreover, they had become integral parts of the university enterprise as they moved into and out of the central faculty of arts and sciences. As an example of this, one might cite the university's research and teaching in international relations, which concerned faculty members in the law school as well as in the department of political science. Or one might cite medical teaching and research, which naturally drew upon the university departments of biology and chemistry. Indeed, the association was wider than that between the professional school and the single department. For example, the Yale Law School, an eminently successful one, may properly be described as an advanced school in the social sciences; it has on its faculty professors whose specialties are political science, economics, psychology, sociology, history, and philosophy. Besides training men to be lawyers, it trains many to enter business or public life. More significantly, the law faculty has accepted the university conception of standards and research. But this one case is merely an excellent exemplar of the idea. In medicine, after Johns Hopkins' early lead, Harvard became the pacesetter as the professional school transformed itself into a vast research laboratory in the pure sciences, while it continued to train physicians and surgeons for practice. In time, this was to become the pattern for the great medical schools across the country.

The trend went beyond law and medicine, though less clearly and completely. The theological schools connected with universities drew upon philosophy, psychology, history, and sociology to support their studies and accepted the ideal of scholarship. This could be seen in Chicago, Yale, and Columbia (Union Theological). The engineering and technological schools, such as the Massachusetts Institute of Technology and the California School of Technology, relied upon the physical sciences and became centers of research more interested in the advancement of knowledge in physics, chemistry, and mathematics than in engineering and applied science. There was, too, a comparable movement towards the university idea in other less fully accepted professional schools: the school of business, for instance, drew closer to such departments as economics, political science, psychology, and sociology.

The assumption by the university of a dual function—the training of professionals and the advancement of knowledge—effected a notable improvement in the professional schools, but this improvement was only part of their total achievement in the third and fourth decades of the century. Another major part was the steady improvement of both the standards of admission and the materials and methods of teaching. As the numbers of candidates for admission increased, the great professional schools were able to require the bachelor's degree for admission. They were able also, if they truly wished it, to demand a breadth and quality of education from the applicants that they could not have asked for before the First World War. But the new position of the professional schools had its disadvantages sometimes, as in the case of premedical students who narrowed their undergraduate education disastrously in the not altogether mistaken idea that the medical school, in spite of pious statements to the contrary, really favored early and intense specialization. Only gradually have the medical schools become convinced that the physician needed an education that included much more than the facts of medical science.

The methods of training men in the professions have come a long way since the simple apprenticeship techniques of colonial days, though the best elements of apprenticeship still survive in medicine and to some extent in law. But much else has been added, especially the rich background and foundation for each of these professions in the broad studies of the university. The seminar, the casebook, the laboratory, and the clinic have supplemented the precept and the demonstration experiment. These new devices, always under severe scrutiny and always subject to change, have made our law and medical schools the equal of any in the world in the production of professional men. It is an asset of incalculable value that these schools also think of themselves as full partners with the rest of the university in the advancement of knowledge in their fields.

CHAPTER V | UNIVERSITY STUDIES

Hitherto in this volume we have considered higher education from the point of view of its institutions—their characteristics, their development, their teachers, trustees, and administrators, and their students. The important matter of the fields of knowledge that make up the studies in the college and university has only been referred to in passing, and usually in the large convenient categories of physical sciences, social sciences, and humanities. It is time now to examine more closely the separate subjects that are studied and taught in the colleges and universities and to trace in some detail their recent development. Here again, the part that has been played by science cannot be overestimated. It is appropriate, therefore, to begin this survey of university studies with a consideration of science.

The modern advancement of scientific thought has given the world a new conception of nature, of man, and of man in nature and society. It has enlarged our perspectives in time and space, changed the direction of our most intimate thoughts, altered the habits of our material life, and given us new vistas for speculation and wonder. Science has become the center of thought and power in our time, and it is in the process of revolutionizing higher education.[1] Few areas of man's learning have failed to be affected by scientific thought and its intellectual method for appraising the value of evidence. In the beginning the scientific method was not greatly different from the careful scrutiny of an object or a problem by an intelligent and curious person, the truth of whose observation was validated by its tangibility and visibility. But from this simple procedure the scientific method has grown into a very sophisticated process indeed. It has been perfected through rigorous use in the major fields of science

—physics, chemistry, and biology—and has become the model and pride of scientists in all parts of the world.

In a typical scientific procedure, the imagination of the scientist builds a hypothesis that is tested by all the available facts; the scientist then eliminates all other possible explanations, and if that is successfully done his hypothesis has become a theory, still subject to challenge from evidence that time and further knowledge may bring forth. Sometimes the speculations of the scientist when he deals with things that cannot, so far, be observed have to be ultimately validated by technology, as when the atom bomb was exploded. At this level, science is a purely mental concept that can be unambiguously expressed only by the abstract symbols of mathematics. Though the techniques of testing and proving the validity of a scientific theory may differ from one field of science to another, this is, I believe, the essential scientific method of today, of which the scientists are justifiably proud.

In substance, scope, and depth also science has made immense advances in the last one hundred and fifty years. In contrast to the earlier descriptive account of things and phenomena, science now customarily deals with forces hitherto unimagined; by mathematics and logic it predicts their weight and strength and, in observing their effects, proves their existence as imagined. An example most clear to the layman, perhaps, is in astronomy, as an unseen star or planet is predicted by its effect on other celestial bodies and is later found by the telescope. But how far we have come, also, in our knowledge of physics, the maturest of the sciences, or in our knowledge of genetics since Mendel, or of chemistry since Priestley, or psychology since Helmholtz! Similar examples of progress could be drawn from every scientific field. Perhaps one of the gravest problems in higher education today is the acceleration of scientific ideas. The quantum theory of Planck is succeeded by theories of electrons and the electrical structure of matter, and Einstein's theory of relativity is followed by theories of wave mechanics and by atom smashing. All this is from one field in science, and the end is not yet. The pace is so incredible that sometimes the old-style professor of physics becomes obsolete in his field and is hardly able to instruct his students in matters that they and the generally educated public badly need to know. Formerly a scientific idea would have had fifty to a hundred years to be absorbed and made an essential part of the view of life of intelligent non-scientists; in the twentieth century it is allowed ten or a dozen years at most. The pace that now prevails in science, where one major advance treads upon the heels of another, has caused a grave crisis in communication, for the young scientist today can often talk to no one but his contemporary in his own field, and that only in a highly specialized language.

In this second great scientific revolution, the seminal ideas have come from Europe. If we begin with Darwin's *Origin of Species* (1859), the work that signalizes the beginning of the modern age in science, the roll call of pioneering scientists up to the Second World War is almost entirely made up of continental and English names. Among such scientific figures as Mendel, Pasteur, Maxwell, Hertz, Kelvin, Roentgen, and Curie, only the name of Willard Gibbs among the Americans seems worthy of mention. In the late nineteenth century we were living upon the intellectual capital of Europe, and this condition has continued to a great extent in the twentieth. One has only to recall the origins of such later scientists as Rutherford, J. J. Thomson, Schroedinger, Heisenberg, Planck, Einstein, Bohr, Freud, and Pavlov to realize how few of the seminal minds in science the United States has yet produced. Gradually we have begun to catch up, greatly aided as we have been in the last three decades by distinguished scientific refugees from the revolutions and wars of Europe. It would not be too much to say that the greatest advances in science in the near future will take place in American universities, for progress in basic scientific research in Europe was checked by the war and its consequences, and the United States in the last decade has poured vast sums and enormous energy into the advancement of scientific knowledge. It is to be hoped, however, that our talent for practical application, for turning all ideas to immediate and useful purposes—a great talent in itself—does not overwhelm the genius we may have for original thinking in science upon which the future of humanity may rest. Our temptation is to put scientific research entirely at the service of national defense, health, and prosperity, and as a nation we are extraordinarily adept in applying such ideas to our material progress. We have had ample occasion to see what immense good and immense ill our technological achievements can do.

The object of the natural sciences is to order our knowledge of nature by establishing a working body of laws or theories that have withstood the eroding effect of new facts and discoveries, and have retained their places as the best explanations we have of natural phenomena. Ideally, nature is consistent in its behavior, and a corpus of comprehensive and uniform laws can be formulated—laws that can be best communicated in the universal language of mathematics. This mature condition is nearest to being realized in the physical sciences of astronomy, chemistry, and physics. Here the structure of matter is weighed and analyzed, quantitatively and qualitatively, and its nature determined. Here, too, are studied those forces that affect matter, such as heat, electricity, wave motion, and energy liberated by atomic fission. In the inorganic aspects of nature, these things are mainly the concern of chemistry and physics; but modern scientific research has gone far towards blurring the line between organic and inorganic, and the discoveries and theories of physics and chemistry reach far into that other major division of the natural sciences, the life sciences. Hence we have in recent decades seen the fruitful development of those areas of knowledge that lie between the conventional disciplines. These are biophysics, biochemistry, microbiology, and molecular biology, as well as geophysics, geochemistry, and paleobotany, which use all the appropriate methods of research established by the traditional studies.

The life sciences, primarily botany and zoology, have not yet attained the maturity of the physical sciences, possibly because the material dealt with is alive and less tractable. But these sciences have used the same rigorous scientific method as the physical sciences and have undergone a comparable development. The life sciences also demand that each premise be validated and that each conclusion stand the rigorous test of new evidence. They have moved from the simple processes of collection and classification used by the early botanists to such theoretical and speculative problems in the study of heredity as the arrangement of the genes. Like other sciences, biology has grown in diversity; and as in physics or chemistry, numbers of specialists now make up a university faculty in the subject, each an expert in a small segment of the field. Working together in teams and often calling upon specialists in physics or chemistry, these scientists formulate workable theories and collect principles, but they must often be content with partial and tentative answers. Still, in looking to the future one may conjecture with some assurance that the next spectacular advances in scientific knowledge may well come in the biological field, and especially in those areas where biological knowledge is employed in conjunction with chemistry and physics. In the meantime, biology is working closely with medical research and providing a solid scientific base for the advancement of knowledge in that field, as well as for the training of physicians. And in those universities, such as Cornell and Wisconsin, where there are large and flourishing schools of agriculture the research and teaching of the life sciences has assumed great proportions and importance. But, indeed, so immediate is the relevance of this study to the health of man that every university of any consequence has striven to make its biological sciences strong.

Physics, chemistry, and biology are the core of the natural sciences, but no comment would be at all satisfactory that did not mention a few of the significant developments in other sciences. The remarkable extension of knowledge that has taken place in astronomy and geology in the twentieth century has become a matter of public interest. With the help of physics and mathematics, speculative theories concerning the age, structure, temperature, composition, and motion of celestial bodies have been formulated and then verified by observation in the gigantic and intricate telescopes we now have. A very high level of predictability has been attained. At the other end of the scale, experimental psychology has found out by experiments upon animal life a great deal about behavior and the process of learning. Theories have been formulated and tested dealing with the location and function of separate parts of the brain and the mechanisms by which behavior is achieved and controlled. A statement by an eminent experimental psychologist says much in a single sentence about one aspect of psychology: "The thinker is viewed as a complex information-processing system." These studies are as yet young but, because they adhere to the rigorous methods of science and have attracted able men, one may reasonably expect many astonishing results in new knowledge touching upon human behavior.

The sciences, then, amply supported in late years by such government agencies as the National Science Foundation and the National Institutes of Health, among others, have valiantly striven through their research to make our world intelligible. Their method has been to find as many uniform, fixed patterns and principles of nature as possible, endlessly testing and refining them towards truth. But in the universities science also has other functions to perform. At the undergraduate level the values inherent in the scientific method—tough-mindedness, awareness, honesty, patience, persistence, and imagination of a special kind—are vital parts of a modern liberal education. And though other disciplines teach these intellectual habits, they are not often as effective as the natural sciences in doing so. In the matter of scientific substance and content, it is difficult to see how a rational modern philosophy can be constructed without a firm and broad knowledge of the present conclusions of the sciences. This is not to say that everyone needs to know the technology and detail of these subjects. It has been well said by a friend of the sciences, "The prospects for a liberal society depend upon the teaching of science as part of a liberal education which is dominated neither by a narrow utilitarianism nor by a comparably myopic professionalism."[2] Perhaps one of the most valuable qualities the student can gain from study of the sciences is the habit of weighing and judging the worth of the evidence presented. For the whole university, one of the most valuable services the sciences perform is to keep the academic community constantly aware of the necessity to be in contact with reality, a characteristic not always present in other studies. It should be added that other studies in their turn may often have a salutary effect upon the practitioners of science.

The pervasive effect of science should be mentioned briefly here—the influence of the scientific method on other fields of knowledge. Where the scientific method has been thoroughly understood, the effect has seldom been harmful. But many other disciplines, imitating science inappropriately to their nature and substance, and obsessed with the idea that facts in themselves are of first and ultimate importance, have been crippled or made unnecessarily dull and earth-bound by their admiration and false emulation of science. This tendency is not only true of some of the disciplines in the social sciences that cannot use the scientific method, but it also may be seen harmfully at work in some of the humanities. That the methods of science are misunderstood is not altogether the fault of the sciences.

The social sciences in their modern elaborated form are late comers to the academic scene.[3] It was the Darwinian idea of evolution as applied to society that provided the stimulus for the development of the full panoply of the social sciences as we now have them in our universities, and Herbert Spencer was its major and seminal spokesman. The triumph of the elective system and the full acceptance of the natural sciences into the curriculum cleared the way for such a development. Early in the twentieth century William Graham Sumner was the foremost American scholar in the general field of social studies as he moved from a moralistic conception of social behavior to a theoretical one and produced the doctrine he called "the science of society." It was no accident that Sumner in the beginning of his career was an ordained minister. The founding of the Social Science Research Council in 1923 marked the coming to maturity of the group of studies devoted to the study of the collective life of man in all its aspects. The academic disciplines included in the large and heterogeneous collection now called the behavioral sciences are anthropology, sociology, social psychology, economics, political science, geography, and most recently linguistics. Sociology, the bellwether of the new social studies, was in search of a method appropriate to these new areas and found one in the use of statistics, measuring the habits and behavior of man quantitatively. The Lynds' analysis of "Middletown" is an excellent example of the statistical method of studying a community that became widely used. Such studies were in line with the prevailing American philosophy of pragmatism, as developed by James and Dewey, and endeavored to attain the impersonality and objectivity of research achieved in the natural sciences. Of course, such a close approach to final proof of a theory was never possible in the social sciences, but the method was applied in varying degrees and ways in all of these disciplines. Where experiments cannot be made, however, it has frequently been necessary to accept approximate answers to social problems. Indeed, some doubt has been expressed by scholars who are not behavioral scientists whether the quantification, classification, and verification by statistics is the most important aspect of such studies as sociology, political science, and psychology. In reaction to philosophical theory, the social sciences at first placed too high a value upon facts for their own sake; but in their later development interpretation, now guided by empirical methods, has re-entered social studies, and occasionally one can detect a profound underlying moral concern.

In their newer aspects, the social sciences first flourished in those universities that were most influenced by scientific research in Germany, such as Hopkins and somewhat later Harvard and Columbia. Because they came so close to the immediate business of everyday life, the social studies were strongly developed in a number of the state universities. An example of this may be seen in the flourishing of political science in Wisconsin in the progressive era, when the elder La Follette put the university to work on political and governmental problems. The greatest development of the social sciences before the Second World War, however, took place at the University of Chicago, where great strength was maintained in economics, political science, anthropology, geography, and psychology. Since the end of the war Chicago, though still strong in the social sciences, has been rivaled by Columbia, Harvard, California, and Stanford. The whole field also, as in the natural sciences, has been undergoing a process of melding into one or two comprehensive units, larger than the conventional disciplines. We may see this trend at Harvard or in the center for behavioral sciences at Palo Alto.

The social or behavioral sciences operate in two related but different ways. Because they deal so directly with the everyday affairs of man's life in society, they are concerned with the application of facts and theories to those everyday interests. The public is well acquainted with this aspect of the behavioral sciences and is sometimes inclined to think, unfairly, that these studies prove the obvious. At a more fundamental level, the behavioral sciences are engaged in the careful and dispassionate attempt to construct, test, and establish a corpus of principles and theories relating to society, to human desires and possibilities. The ultimate aim is to refine our conception of human nature and to describe more precisely the total human society.

As in the natural sciences, the development of experts and specialists in the social sciences has led to an ever increasing participation by these men in the affairs of the nation. In the peace conferences after the First World War, a few professors, mainly historians and what we now call political scientists, were used by our government in the negotiations. In the catastrophe of the great depression, many economists from the universities were taken into President Roosevelt's

Brain Trust; they were later joined by a number of political scientists. In the Second World War the whole range of social scientists was engaged: anthropologists and geographers were called upon for their knowledge of the peoples and lands of the Pacific; economists and political scientists were in demand by the gatherers and analysts of intelligence for the production and control of arms and goods and for the management of Lend Lease programs; psychologists were pressed into service for the development of propaganda. During the war, too, it was found useful for military people who were to operate in distant areas of the earth to be trained in a combination of language and several of the social sciences, in programs known as area studies. Thus comprehensive programs were established to provide a knowledge of the language and the social institutions of such areas as the Far East, Southeast Asia, and the Soviet Union. Since the war such studies have been continued in refined and improved form, for the government realized that the new position of the United States among the nations required a constant supply of men with a knowledge of the language and way of life of many countries. Strong university centers have consequently maintained and augmented their language and area programs for China, Japan, Southeast Asia, India, the Near East, and the Soviet Union, and recently such studies have been extended to Africa. Moreover, since the end of the war social scientists of every kind have been sent to all parts of the globe to assist in such programs of foreign aid as the Marshall Plan and the Point Four Program, as the country took its place in the new arrangements of the nations.

Increasingly, too, local government and industry have drawn upon the professors of the several social sciences. Such men are in demand as analysts of the efficiency of industry, as directors of state or regional economy, as tax experts, and as arbitrators in labor disputes. They have been engaged as advisers in the problems of urban renewal, conservation, and transportation. If the prime duty of the university was to serve the immediate, pressing needs of the country and the community, the social sciences were surely studies to be highly prized. In the 1940s and 1950s the great philanthropic foundations saw in the rapid development of the social sciences the quick and ready cure for many of the ills of society. The Carnegie and Ford foundations for a period devoted the great bulk of their resources to these studies and activities; in this they faithfully reflected the temper of the country at the time. The sciences, especially the physical sciences it was thought, would be amply taken care of by the government, and the biological and medical sciences could look after themselves. Since those days expectation of immediate improvement through the social sciences has somewhat diminished perhaps, as it has become clearer that the cures provided for social ills are usually of short range, applicable only to specific conditions and ineffective when those conditions change. This comment is hardly just to the social sciences, for their relevance to immediate problems is at once their weakness and their strength. But gradually out of experience a set of common principles and procedures is being developed in these studies, upon which each discipline is erecting techniques appropriate to itself.

Economics, the oldest of the social sciences, has naturally fed in the last century upon the enormous development of industry, business, and government. With ever greater experience to call upon and continuous records for its guidance, economics has employed new techniques to objectify, to measure more precisely, economic phenomena in order to control and if possible to predict developments. This has led to the elaboration of the subject into the study of all aspects of economic activity and life, from the production and distribution of the national income to business cycles and labor unions, from industrial structure to government financing, from the economics of underdeveloped areas to the comparison of economic systems, from money and credit to economic history. It has also led to econometrics and the immensely greater use of computers and technology, as vast quantities of data are processed in machines. Perhaps more nearly than any other social study, economics approaches the surer condition of a science, though in the nature of its material it can never arrive at the certainty of prediction that the natural sciences at their best attain. Like the natural sciences, the study of economics in Europe was well ahead of its progress in the United States in point of time, and so far this country has not contributed many major seminal ideas. Thorstein Veblen did develop a new version of economic behavior in his *Theory of the Leisure Class,* but the idea that has dominated economic thought in recent decades has come from the Englishman, John Maynard Keynes.[4] Keynesian economics, devoted to the idea of the control of economic trends through spending by the government, has of course been under sharp attack from conservative economists and advocates of private enterprise. This has been especially true in America as economic conditions have improved; but no comparable large idea has come to take its place, and Keynesian economics continues to dominate the study in American universities. During the last few decades, strong departments of economics have risen in every part of the country, and important centers of research and economic thought have flourished at Harvard, Columbia, California (Berkeley), and latterly at Yale. But it is invidious to name only a few eminent departments; at present there are possibly a dozen very strong centers in the country.

Political science, in part a natural extension of history, has undergone the kind of development that may be seen in several of the social sciences. The discipline has risen from philosophical theory, drawn from Greece and Rome, to the empirical study of political institutions and parties, power groups, international relations, comparative government, and political behavior. In the nature of things, there cannot be very much science in this study. A strenuous effort, however, is steadily made to use the tools of psychology to establish constants of political behavior in large as well as in small groups. This effort has been furthered by the establishment by the Ford Foundation of the institute for the study of social behavior at Palo Alto, where scholars in the social sciences can spend extended periods of time consulting with colleagues and deliberating and developing their special interests. There can be little doubt that the books written, the knowledge amassed in the area of political affairs, and the counsel given have been decidedly useful to the federal and local governments; especially is this true in the study of the structures, traditions, and actions of foreign governments. Departments of political science in strong colleges and universities have also been of much service to the government in training personnel for civil and foreign service. Among the universities Chicago was again pre-eminent before and during the Second World War, but more recently several other leading universities have challenged its priority in the field, the most recent of which are Yale and Princeton.

Standing apart from economics and political science, which have sometimes been called policy sciences, is a group of disciplines in the social sciences that are more concerned with the organization, structure, and functioning of society, sometimes drawing close to study of the individual man. These are psychology, sociology, and anthropology, subjects very close to each other, but each emphasizing aspects of social behavior peculiar to itself.

Since the beginning of the present century, the new psychology has profoundly affected every phase of modern thought and feeling. The public is steadily aware of its influence, in diluted form of course; but its deeper impact on other fields of learning, such as literature, history, religion, and art, can only be fully appreciated by experts in those fields. Beginning in the old classical curriculum as "mental philosophy," the discipline in modern times has bifurcated into two major divisions: experimental psychology, which is closest to zoology and physiology and customarily uses animals for experimental purposes, and social psychology, which analyzes large social influences upon behavior and is concerned with such matters in the individual as achievement, conformity, or frustration. Within these large divisions many smaller specialties have developed, and psychologists are at work upon processes and problems that concern the brain: learning, thinking, motivation, communication. These matters are considered in the mass as well as in their implications for individuals. Psychology as a study includes many special fields: child development, personality, abnormal psychology, tests and measurements, and statistics, not to mention the special aspects of psychology in such activities as education and administration.

Obviously, the experimental aspect of psychology comes nearest to meeting the rigorous definition of the scientific method as it operates in the physical sciences. Elsewhere, the theories or principles of psychological behavior are approximate generalizations, as is the case in the Kinsey statistics on sexual habits. Modern psychology received its great stimulus in recent times from Freud's studies of the unconscious; how scientific his methods were may be debated, but he is surely one of the seminal thinkers of this century. His ideas were elaborated by Jung into the theory of the collective unconscious, an idea that is influential today in the study of literature. More distinctly scientific work in psychology was accomplished by Pavlov, with his methods of investigating the nervous systems of animals. In America little fresh thought has been added to the subject since the valuable *Principles of Psychology* of William James in 1890 and his *Varieties of Religious Experience* in 1902. During the 1920s the behaviorist movement in psychology was begun by John Broadus Watson. Behaviorism flourished vigorously for a while, but in the next decade faded as a major force though it remained influential. It was peculiarly American in its pragmatic and empirical procedures. The psychologists of this country have developed and refined clinical psychology and psychiatry, and this has profoundly affected the study of medicine. Though not as numerous as great departments of physics or economics, distinguished departments of psychology may be found in most of the eminent universities of the country and frequently may be seen cooperating closely with excellent schools of medicine.

Sociology and anthropology, concerned with the behavior of human beings in groups, are the furthest of the behavioral sciences from physics in the application of the scientific method, and the closest to the humanities in their procedures. Through observation, experience, and appeal to public verification by an accumulation of cases, these studies aim to establish durable generalizations. Their implements are statistics and analysis—methods by which these sciences have gathered a large store of tested information, useful not only for understanding the cultures and institutions of many societies, but also in enabling the individual man to know his condition and where he stands among his fellows.

Sociology, defined as the scientific analysis of social phenomena, took its rise from theological and philosophical thought. But it developed in response to the acute social problems of a society in transition from a rural habit of life to an industrial one. The task sociology faced in the twentieth century was to make an empirical, scientific study of man in the mass, his organizations and institutions, the large movements that affect social conditions, and the responses that men make to these movements. Rising out of settlement work and other earnest efforts to improve local conditions, sociology has striven to generalize the results of its analysis by comparative investigations, and by that means to find the causes beneath the facts. The task was huge and not clearly delineated; the problem was to perfect, if possible, a reliable method of attack. The theorizing of Sumner, though highly intelligent, did not get down to cases. There developed gradually the idea of the empirical study of communities—to be seen at its classic best in *Middletown*, the Lynds' analysis of Muncie, Indiana,[5] a work followed by similar studies of cities in other parts of the nation. Studies were also made of the process of social change, as in Ogburn's *Social Change*, of rural sociology by Odum and Vance in North Carolina, and of population and ecology and other elements of social behavior. The sexual behavior of men and women was investigated by Kinsey, using interviews, samplings, and statistics to arrive at his generalizations. Though the method in all these studies was not scientifically precise, the information gathered was often most useful, shedding light on such other social sciences as economics, politics, and psychology, and providing materials for the use of lawmakers, historians, philosophers, and novelists. The studies by David Riesman of the individual caught in urban industrial society add a further dimension to sociology.[6] The University of Chicago was the early leader in the development of sociology in its modern form, but in recent years Chicago has had to share its eminence in this field with Columbia, Harvard, and other institutions in the South and West.

Anthropology, the science of man, has especially concerned itself with the investigation of preliterate peoples and also with prehistoric man. The subject has been split into two major parts, physical and cultural anthropology. Physical anthropology is involved in measuring and describing the structural features of the races of man, ancient and modern, and classifying men and races into types. The study has aroused a great deal of public interest in matters of race and ethnography, and by its serious scholarship has greatly clarified the prehistory of man, especially of European man.[7] Recently, physical anthropology has extended its attention in point of time and geography as fossils of prehistoric man have been discovered in many parts of the world. It has also been interested in types of living men as shown by physical structure, or the composition of the hair or blood, and the indications these attributes have for temperament and personality. Cultural anthropology is dissociated from the biological aspects of man and deals rather with the languages, customs, and institutions of tribes and races. It is mainly descriptive of primitive people in all parts of the world. Cultural anthropology cannot attain the precision required of the scientific method, but through its observation and careful analysis it has gathered innumerable facts about human behavior and has arrived at many valuable generalizations. This aspect of anthropology was of great use during the Second World War, and since then more than a dozen American universities have banded together in an organization, the Human Relations Area Files, to collect information about the peoples of the world. In the field of anthropology at large, the United States has been a pioneer and one of the leaders, and strong centers have been established in some dozen leading universities.

These studies, then, are the central disciplines in the social or behavioral sciences. Other closely related subjects show a similar evolution from observation, common sense, speculation, and philosophy as they move towards more precise validation, usually by empirical and comparative methods. An example of this may be seen in the broad area of geography. The early theories of Ellsworth Huntington upon climate and its effect upon man, and those of Semple upon the places of man's settlement, have given way to more exact studies of location, ecology, meteorology, resources, and political divisions. The development of the social sciences in this country, moreover, has provided a firm base for the study of law and has profoundly affected the modern conception of its origin, nature, and validity. By reason of the findings of psychology and sociology, the theory of law has moved from a dogmatic formulation of theology and morality, tradition and custom, to a much more flexible consideration of the psychology of man and the conditions of his life. At present, the prevailing idea is that law has evolved from man in society and must change to meet that continuing evolution. To a great extent, the modern law school is an advanced school of the social sciences. Medical schools have also made important use of psychology and sociology and have added departments devoted to the psychiatric and sociological aspects of medicine.

One point, made in an earlier chapter, may be restated here. With the decline of public interest in theology and the loss of faith in dogma, the problems raised by tolerance and intolerance have shifted. Today, the matters of greatest concern for most people are social beliefs and loyalties. The issue of academic freedom has accordingly changed its causes, and today the teacher is challenged for his political, economic, or social opinions. This fact is one indication of the vitality of these studies and evidence of how closely they touch the national and the individual life. The dispassionate and objective analysis of matters so deeply affecting life and vital interests now often outrages members of society quite as much as new or unorthodox religious ideas formerly did.

The third and oldest conventional division of university studies is the humanities, and here the central disciplines are history, literature, and philosophy. Of increasing importance, too, in recent decades has been the study of the fine arts and music. History, literature, and philosophy form the core of liberal studies in the colleges and maintain their places at more advanced and professional levels in the graduate schools. Each of these disciplines, in spite of its long traditions, has been affected by the scientific temper of the age, and each has had to reassert its own integrity and to reaffirm or develop its own methods. The basic concern of these studies is for the individual, in contrast to that of the sciences which is for nature and that of the social sciences which is for society or man in the mass. Far more than the other divisions of knowledge, the humanities are involved in the definition of values, and they exercise a supervision upon the moral and intellectual qualities of man's actions and thoughts. The materials in which the humanities deal are mainly of the past, but it is the task of the interpreter of these studies to use them to give significance and direction to the present and the future. Through the centuries these studies have fed the imagination of individual man, nourished his personality, and strengthened his faith in his freedom.

History, the most comprehensive of subjects, looks both to the humanities and to the social sciences. In its older form, as it dealt with the lives of great persons and entertained literary aspirations, it was distinctly one of the humanities. It still has those elements and a special care for the individual, his freedoms and obligations, and his effect upon the course of events. But history also deals with man in society; it is the tale of nations and movements and in this respect is near the social sciences. At the end of the nineteenth century the subject was firmly established as a proper academic study, but its primary concern was with the political and military history of the ancient world, Europe, and America. In the twentieth century the fragmentation and specialization of the subject has been spectacular and is still developing. Not only has each nation, region, and city its political, social, and intellectual history, but so has every age and, in the centers of civilization where such ample records are now kept, so does every decade, every institution, and every movement. Inevitably, the number of specialists in the universities has increased greatly, and studies of all kinds and sizes pour from the scholarly presses.

In the early part of this century, the study of history fell under the spell of science, or rather of a misunderstanding of scientific procedures and effects. Profoundly impressed by the Darwinian doctrine of evolution, most historians of the time thought that facts, meticulously collected and set down chronologically, impersonally, and impartially, would speak for themselves as they fell into an intelligible pattern. Historians were obsessed by fact, and the old literary impressionistic historians, Gibbon, Carlyle, Macaulay, and Parkman, were anathema. But the historians of larger minds, aware of the new horizons disclosed by Freud and Einstein, and aware also of developments in anthropology, archaeology, and prehistory, began to see that the facts did not speak for themselves, but had to be interpreted. Charles Beard early, and Carl Becker more tellingly, pointed out the incapacity of unselected and uninterpreted facts to capture the life and spirit of an historical event or time. As Becker said in "Everyman His Own Historian," in the *American Historical Review* in 1932:

Since history is not a part of the external material world, but an imaginative reconstruction of vanished events, its form and substance are inseparable; in the realm of literary discourse substance, being an idea, *is* form; and form, conveying the idea, *is* substance. It is thus not the undiscriminated fact, but the perceiving mind of the historian that speaks; the special meaning which facts are made to convey emerges from the substance-form, which the historian employs to recreate imaginatively a series of events not present to perception.[8]

Every generation must reinterpret history for its own purposes, of course—for its understanding of the past and its expectations of the future—and in the hands of conscientious historians the matter is safe. But that it can be a weapon in the hands of partisans or manipulators of men and nations we may see in the writing and rewriting of history in Russia and Germany. At its best history is the conscientious "caretaker of the past," as it has been called, and gives society and individuals perspective and stability in the presence of change and chance. The modern historian has abandoned the impressionistic writing of the nineteenth century but, careful and conscientious as he is in his handling of facts, he is not a scientist. History is an art, and its value to man is moral rather than scientific since it deepens the sympathies, fortifies the will, and liberalizes the mind. It is also a store of wisdom for the public use as it warns against excesses and the pressures of the moment.

The study of history has flourished in the United States, and a few of the most influential ideas and works in the field in the late nineteenth and early twentieth centuries should be recorded here. F. J. Turner's essay, "The Significance of the Frontier in American History" (1893),[9] has had an immense influence on the writers of American history, though it may be that the heavy emphasis on this one idea has obscured the consideration of other elements in the development of this country. In 1913 Beard, perhaps influenced by the thinking of Marx, proposed an economic interpretation of history that, though it did not escape challenge, was admired and extremely influential for a time. Wallace Notestein introduced the concept of social history; and Michael Rostovtzeff became the economic historian of the ancient world. Philosophical and intellectual history found a talented spokesman in Becker, whose *Heavenly City of the Eighteenth Century Philosophers* (1932) is a landmark. Intellectual history has flourished in this country in the hands of such scholars as Ralph Gabriel, Perry Miller, Crane Brinton, and Richard Hofstadter; and social and regional studies are well represented by

Oscar Handlin, David Potter, and C. Vann Woodward. Mention should be made, too, of the massive and altogether admirable histories of American universities, which may be seen at their best in Samuel Eliot Morison's account of Harvard, George W. Pierson's of Yale, and Merle Curti's of Wisconsin. Comprehensive histories of American education are few; among them George Schmidt's work on the liberal colleges, John Brubacher's on the universities, and Frederick Rudolph's on both deserve mention.[10] The most recent development in historical studies is the extension of the field to include new territories: the Far and Near East, the Middle East, Africa, Russia, and Eastern Europe. To provide for these studies, as well as the more established ones, a few great universities have taken on the task: in the East, Harvard, Columbia, Yale, Cornell, and Princeton; in the Midwest, Michigan and Chicago; in the Far West, California (Berkeley and Los Angeles), Washington, and Stanford. The only regret to be recorded in the matter of historical study in this country is the decline of the comprehensive study of Greece and Rome—though much is being done in archaeology—and of a few of the countries of contemporary Europe. There are not enough good scholars to meet all the needs.

A second great study in the humanities is literature, and like every other major field it has become specialized and professionalized during the twentieth century. Like other subjects, too, literature has expanded its interests to include new areas and new methods. By the beginning of the present century, professional associations had been established, and learned journals dedicated to research in the field were being published.[11] The major fact concerning literary studies in the twentieth century is that English literature, along with American, has taken the central place in university studies that was formerly occupied by Greek and Latin literature. No doubt this change had to be made in the interest of democratic education, but the partial dissociation from European culture that is a consequence is not entirely compensated for by the increase in the study of modern

European languages and literatures. Nevertheless, it must be said that English and American literature have provided a valuable binding element in the national culture. In the United States, at any rate, it has been literature written in English which has assumed the function that literature customarily performs—to train the mind, the emotions, the sensibilities, the imagination, the taste, and the conscience of the student. Literature is a maturing subject, appropriately taught in the college curriculum but, in its many subtleties and problems, reaching into the graduate school and beyond. It is an essential ingredient in the education of the individual. Because English and American literature holds a central position in college and university studies in this country, I shall trace briefly its development in the twentieth century.[12]

At the beginning of the century, the professional study of English literature was in the process of transforming itself from the older belleletristic appreciation into a rigorous and scientific investigation, as far as this was possible. The many young Americans returning from the German universities had a vision of philology, literature treated "genetically" in the spirit of science in order to show sources, connections, and relationships. The facts of literary history and the biographies of writers were of great importance and had not been systematically collected for English literature. Immense quantities of facts were therefore gathered and published in articles and small books. Texts and reliable editions were made. Early English literature was a favorite field, perhaps because the German universities had begun to cultivate it.[13] This work was often pedantic and trivial, but sometimes it was solid and useful,[14] and later scholars are much in its debt. In general, the early practitioners of philology were notably lacking in aesthetics and critical criteria. They knew everything about a poem except why it was poetry. To obtain the necessary rigor in the training of their students, they imposed such language requirements as Gothic, Old Norse, and Old French.

In the study of literature, unlike science, the new does not obliterate the old; and philological studies continue to exist as new

approaches to literature have evolved. Philology became more sophisticated and discriminating, though, as one may see in such
works as J. L. Lowes's *The Road to Xanadu* (1927), C. B. Tinker's
The Young Boswell (1922), or J. W. Krutch's *Samuel Johnson* (1944).
An increasingly exacting standard of professional work may be seen
in handbooks devoted to major authors. The most noticeable development of philological scholarship in later decades, however, is to be
seen in the large editions, often done by a team of scholars, of the
works of Spenser, Milton, Shakespeare, Sir Thomas More, Boswell,
and Walpole. This work is generally of the highest competence and
has been until recently America's characteristic product in literary
studies. It is not too much to say that in such philological activity the
scholars of this country have not only outdistanced Germany, but
have outstripped Britain as well.

It was inevitable that there would be an intellectual rebellion
against the early kind of philological study, for the philologists
were inclined to worship facts and had no critical or moral criteria in
their procedures. The rebellion started with a group of scholars who
came to be known as the New Humanists, led by Irving Babbitt and
Paul Elmer More. The temper of these men was classical, and for
their standards and criteria they referred to classical ideals and
authors. They strove to introduce a moralistic element into the study
of literature and were in themselves austere ethical rationalists. They
were conservative and aristocratic, and abstract in their thinking.
They were never popular, even among professors of literature, but
their influence was profound in special places. T. S. Eliot was trained
in this school and admired it until he found it too pagan for his
religious convictions. The movement rested on Babbitt's books: *Literature and the American College* (1908), *Masters of Modern French
Criticism* (1912), and *Rousseau and Romanticism* (1912), and also
on More's early work in his *Shelburne Essays* (1904–1921). Later
these pioneers were joined by Norman Forester whose work in this
kind, *The American Scholar*, appeared in 1929. The humanists spoke
for reason and proportion, and against the irrationalities and in-

dulgences of their day, especially romanticism. With all their serious purpose and critical acumen, these men lacked catholicity of taste and were hostile to contemporary art and literature. After 1930 the movement died, but its ideas had penetrated deeply into the minds of a number of important literary people and had influenced literary standards.

In the hard years of the depression it was inevitable that there should have been concern about the social situation and that this concern should express itself in a point of view towards literature. The Marxist approach to literature is employed in Granville Hicks's *Figures of Transition* (1939), a work that stressed the familiar doctrine of economic determinism. There was little learning in Hicks's criticism, and not much force; indeed, the Marxist view had very little effect on literary criticism. A more influential body of opinion, indebted to the principles of Jeffersonian democracy, was to be found in Vernon Parrington's *Main Currents of American Thought* (1927–1930). But Parrington was so interested in social thought that he tended to neglect literature, and as times improved his work fell into disuse. Social and political concern, however, was more permanent, and in a form indebted primarily to neither Marx nor Jefferson, it appears in such different works as Edmund Wilson's *Axel's Castle* (1931) and Lionel Trilling's study of Matthew Arnold (1939).

In the same decade a more significant movement for literature began to flourish in this country, though its origins in Europe were much earlier. This was known as the History of Ideas. Early works with this approach to literature began to appear in the twenties,[15] but the movement began in force with A. O. Lovejoy's *The Great Chain of Being* (1936) and continued with J. W. Beach's *Concept of Nature in Nineteenth Century Poetry* (1936), R. F. Jones's *Ancients and Moderns* (1936), Douglas Bush's two volumes, *Mythology and the Renaissance Tradition in English Poetry* (1932) and *Mythology and the Romantic Tradition in English Poetry* (1937), and Perry Miller's *The New England Mind* (1939), to name only a few samples of an active and continuing approach to literature. This kind of study requires much erudition and a subtle perception in detecting relationships. Drawing upon all phases of intellectual and cultural history, it is in itself an exacting study and has often proved helpful in the interpretation of literature. It has attracted many able scholars. The shortcomings of this kind of study of literature may be seen in Lovejoy. He was by profession a philosopher and his approach to literature was exclusively intellectual, but his analysis of the ideas he found in a work almost destroyed it as literature. Poetry to him was a document, and there was little sympathy for a work of the imagination. Perhaps the major deficiency of the history of ideas as a method of literary study is that there is no innate necessity for criteria of value and judgment. A poor poem in the history of ideas may be as valuable as a great one: Erasmus Darwin's "Loves of the Triangles" is as important as Milton's "Lycidas."

Since the Second World War, the dominant movement in literary scholarship and teaching in this country has been the New Criticism. The name of the movement came from a book with that title, published in 1941 by John Crowe Ransom. Its origin, however, was in I. A. Richards' two volumes, *Principles of Literary Criticism* (1924) and *Practical Criticism* (1929). Ransom's book discussed the major practitioners of the new method, Richards, T. S. Eliot, and Yvor Winters. The term New Critic covers such a wide variety of American scholars as Ransom, Cleanth Brooks, R. P. Blackmur, Kenneth Burke, and F. O. Matthiessen, and abroad such a critic as William Empson. After Ransom, the most important advocates of the new criticism were Brooks and Matthiessen, whose works stress the study of imagery, texture, and symbolism in a poem.[16] It is probable that the textbook, *Understanding Poetry*, by Brooks and Robert Penn Warren has been the most effective disseminator of the ideas and methods of the new critics. At any rate, the comment of Brooks in 1943 that the new critics "have next to no influence in the universities"[17] has long been out of date—every English department in the country is well staffed with them and their heirs. In spite of the name, the method of study is an old one, and its novelty lies in its emphatic reinstatement in this century.

The new critics, rebelling against the easy, impressionistic habits of reading that had become prevalent, and acutely dissatisfied with the methods of literary study that applied no standards of value, insisted upon close scrutiny of a piece of literature. They concentrated upon the text, analyzing the diction, images, symbols, the texture, rhythm, and structure in order to discover the secrets of a poem's effectiveness and to appraise its value. They looked for the unity of a piece of literature, its coherence and maturity. They strove to isolate it from extraneous considerations—its background in history, biography, or the literary tradition. They were often interested in the social and political ideas or the religious and ethical ones reflected in literature, but above all they were interested in the aesthetic fact and were absorbed in the study of ambiguities, ironies, and images.

The scholars who come under the rubric of new criticism are so diverse that it is difficult to appraise the group as a whole. Many virtues of the movement are apparent. First, the reader was led back to the literary work itself. Next, the new critics were concerned with problems of value, a concern that the philologists, the historians of ideas, and the social critics seldom exhibited. Further, they were young men in contact with the active world and saw the problems of life directly, and not as abstract ideas. The movement resuscitated the study of literature in America at a time when revitalizing was badly needed.

There were obvious shortcomings, however. In their zeal the new critics were neglectful, often scornful, of other methods of scholarship and failed to appreciate what historical research, for example, could do. Only internal evidence was admissible. Possibly this is why the new critics like to deal with poems of our own day, for here the background may be taken for granted. More seriously, the new critics exhibit certain limitations in range, for they favor literature where the procedures they cherish will work best. They prefer the short poem of the seventeenth century or the present and are noticeably less successful with longer works, the drama or the novel. They leave untreated enormous portions of English literature. Further, each of the critics has tended to develop a special vocabulary, which has discouraged many readers of poetry and criticism. Finally, the less wise of the new critics have become obsessed with the appurtenances of poetry to the exclusion of its broader and more important aspects. New criticism has matured and is at its best when it operates in partnership with other kinds of literary scholarship, as it does in such works as Walter J. Bate's *The Stylistic Development of Keats* (1945), H. M. Abrams' *The Mirror and the Lamp* (1953), and Louis L. Martz's *Poetry of Meditation* (1954).

In the 1960s an old literary interest has been revived in a new form—the search for the archetypal myth or symbol. The origin of this movement may be traced to Carl Jung's *The Psychology of the Unconscious* (1912) where the central doctrine of the "collective unconscious" is presented. In archetypes of legends current in all parts of the world, one may see form, pattern, and recurrent modes of viewing reality. The literary phase of this kind of study was begun by Maud Bodkin in *Archetypal Patterns in Poetry* (1934). Recently, the movement has been reinvigorated by Northrop Frye's brilliant *Anatomy of Criticism* (1957). Attention is called to such universal symbols in poetry as day and night, spring and autumn, birth and death, the garden of innocence and experience, and such legendary figures as Prometheus, Odysseus, Faust, and Satan. The problem is to refrain from seeing such symbols everywhere. As Douglas Bush says so wittily: "Some ideas, such as frustration, became master-keys for opening all doors. A crowd of authors and characters were seen trudging along the road back to the womb. Along a parallel road stumbled another crowd driven by the death wish. Since *Moby Dick* has been a special target for critical theories, one might add the suggestion that the white whale represents the Spirit of Literature turning and reviling the one-legged critics."[18] Illuminating as such a study of archetypal symbols can be, it does not require of the critic any criteria of value.

These, then, have been the major modes of literary study in American universities in this century. But in the broad area there have been other developments that should also be mentioned. First, bibliography has made sharp advances in becoming more professionalized, more accurate and informative, and has learned to employ techniques unknown to our fathers. Next is the great increase of interest in the history of criticism and its better use of knowledge and skills. This revived interest owes much to Croce, and more immediately to T. E. Hulme, Ezra Pound, and T. S. Eliot. In America the resurgence has attracted a number of able scholars, among whom one may name René Wellek, Austin Warren, Harry Levin, and William Wimsatt.[19] The application of critical theory has led to an increasing number of subtle and valuable studies of the style of particular authors and movements.[20] One must also mention two developments of a contradictory kind in recent decades: the enormous increase in the study of American literature, signifying a greater national concern and maturity; and the greater involvement of literary studies in comparative literature as the international horizons of the country widen. Something must also be said about the changing nature of the study of linguistics. From the simpler study of etymologies and the making of dictionaries, the study has moved through more sophisticated stages towards science. Some of its notable American achievements are Sir William Craigie's *Dictionary of American English* (1936–1944), the ambitious *Linguistic Atlas*— showing the origins of the settlers of America through their idioms— begun in the thirties and only now approaching completion, and the scholarly analyses of language by Edward Sapir and Leonard Bloomfield. Language, in the form of structural linguistics, is now studied as a science. Evidence concerning the origin of language and its evolution is drawn from physiology and anthropology, and its characteristics are computed on machines.

A few further miscellaneous observations might be made. The study of the classics has broadened its concern to include the lively modern interest in the archaeology of Greece and Rome and has also welcomed eagerly the widespread curiosity aroused by the Minoan language problems. Neither the scholars of the classics nor those concerned with modern foreign literatures have been deeply affected by the movements in the study of literature that are being employed in the United States, though several of these movements originated in Europe. Perhaps this is because the study is older in Europe and habits have been long set, but partly also it is because Europe has had less leisure and fewer resources to devote to these studies in an era of war.

Though literature is central in the humanities, there are of course other arts whose study has increasingly engaged the scholarship of specialists in the American universities. The history and criticism of the fine arts and music have taken prominent places in the curriculum, and those studies have become more specialized and professional. Moreover, connections have been made between these arts and literature and history, making the whole consideration more sophisticated and interesting. Though these studies in their advanced forms are not as widely pursued as literature, the number and quality of concert halls, galleries, and art libraries have increased as the country has grown wealthier and more conscious of the value of the arts. Interest in the art of Asia and Africa is growing, but the major task of the study of art and music is to catch up with Europe, where these subjects have so long been cultivated. As in science, the maturing of these studies has been greatly aided by the influx of refugees from abroad.

Another central discipline in university studies is the ancient one of philosophy.[21] To follow the progress of this study in the present century is especially instructive, for philosophy reflects faithfully the changing moods and aspirations of the times. At the beginning of the century, the temper of the country was hopeful, expansive, humanitarian, and democratic. The reasons for this mood were several: the continuing effects of the eighteenth-century Enlightenment, the enormous progress of science in the nineteenth century, the industrial prosperity of the country, and the political success of the country at home and abroad. As a result, the prevailing philosophy in most American universities was idealistic, and its eloquent and eminent spokesman was Josiah Royce.[22] Through his major works Royce set forth his conviction that behind the material world and the scientific principle of evolution there exists the spiritual reality of the mind of man. Because of this spiritual reality it could be hoped that the country would move inevitably towards the Great Community of Royce's imagination, and the implement for that progress was the principle of loyalty that every man owed to the institutions of society, to the city and the region of which he was a member, and finally to the national state itself. Noble in itself, the concept was made even more attractive by Royce's skill as an expositor. The trouble with it was that it was so far removed from ordinary life and the changing social forces of the time. Humanity was no closer to realizing the ideal of the Great Community than King Arthur's knights were in living up to the code of the Round Table. But only reluctantly and gradually was the essential inadequacy of this idealistic philosophy recognized. It is not surprising that it lingered longer in the academic world than elsewhere.

To provide a philosophy more relevant to American life as it actually was, and more intellectually satisfactory, a body of thought began to take form even before the beginning of the twentieth century. This new conception, even more representative of the American temper, took its rise in the thinking of William James and Charles Sanders Peirce.[23] For the layman, the new movement may be most easily followed in James's *Principles of Psychology* (1890), where he sought to establish a connection between ideas and direct personal experience. James developed his idea in *The Will to Believe* (1896) and *Some Problems of Philosophy* (1911). In the beginning James was not a full-blown pragmatist, but he gradually moved towards that position and stressed more and more an empirical, down-to-earth conception that may fairly be called by that name. James's pragmatism, a magnanimous personal view of life, was most influential.

It was John Dewey, however, who developed pragmatism in its most professional form and made it the American philosophy par excellence. Writing in 1950 on the effect of pragmatism in America, Henry Steele Commager described it in these words: "Practical, democratic, individualistic, opportunistic, spontaneous, hopeful, pragmatism was wonderfully adapted to the temperament of the average American. . . . No wonder that, despite the broadsides of more formidable philosophers, pragmatism caught on until it became almost the official philosophy of America."[24] Basing his thought upon the scientific method of experiment, Dewey sought to establish positive values as the only reliable way by which we could achieve the goals we hoped for. Dewey believed in the development of the individual, but this development was best attained in a context of social planning. Only by such planning could the conditions necessary for the production of quality be provided. As we have seen in an earlier chapter, Dewey's philosophy was immensely influential and had a profound effect upon American education.

The pragmatic philosophy confirmed and brought to maturity the American concepts of democracy and liberalism before the First World War. The effects of the philosophy may still be seen in the society, and its teachings are still powerful in the universities. In the twenties, though, professional philosophers showed an increasing skepticism concerning the adequacy of pragmatism to satisfy intellectual and spiritual needs, however useful its procedures were in ordinary life. The social sciences, grounded upon the empirical method, became more specialized and objective, and as they did so they abandoned their earlier commitment to values and to social reform. Their methods had undermined their moralistic point of view, and trends and events made their practical ideals seem dubious. Liberalism was challenged by a resurgent traditionalism; democracy began to seem less efficient than the new totalitarianism; and the feverish prosperity of the twenties, followed by the depression of the thirties, caused many to challenge the pragmatic ideals of the nation. The question was asked: "What were the purposes of the Great Community as the pragmatists saw them?"

In the thirties, therefore, both the idealist and the pragmatic philosophies suffered a rapid distintegration. In the universities, as in the country at large, philosophical interests splintered off into many minor movements, such as technocracy and the managerial revolution. There was a widespread skepticism about traditional values. Two more movements of some size, in contradiction to each other, made some headway. Marxism found few advocates in the universities, but appealed to a number of younger men as a way out of the country's economic and political dilemma.[25] More respectable as a philosophy was the so-called medieval revival, led by Etienne Gilson.[26] This movement was Christian and Catholic, dogmatic and traditional, and was grounded upon a faith in supernatural revelation whose interpreter was the Church. It offered as a solution to the prevailing chaos an order in nature and the affairs of men as formulated by Aristotle and the church fathers, especially Thomas Aquinas. Its best expositors were European by birth and temperament. In America its philosophical effect was not great, but its success in higher education, as we have seen, was more substantial. Here Robert Maynard Hutchins was its ablest advocate.

But even as these modes of thought strove to establish themselves in the vacuum left by the failure of pragmatism, academic philosophers were busy developing a system that was to be more lasting, one that occupies an important place in philosophical study today. The new men were so-called realists, who strove to see things as they are, freed from subjective opinions. They undertook to merge logic and mathematics and applied the methods of science to secure the necessary rigorous discipline. The leaders in this movement were Alfred North Whitehead and Bertrand Russell, who collaborated on the seminal work *Principia Mathematica*, published in three volumes in 1910–1913. Through a refined and specialized analysis they hoped to gain clarity, accuracy, and intellectual honesty. Other philosophers —Arthur O. Lovejoy and Morris Raphael Cohen—refined and matured the movement.[27] In America Whitehead was the leading spokesman, and he constructed a system of metaphysics based on philosophical reason in his series of volumes, *Science and the Modern World* (1925), *Adventures in Ideas* (1933), and *Modes of Thought* (1938). His system of thought was eclectic, liberal, and romantic, and the result was a sane statement that appealed both to professional philosophers and to laymen.

Out of the joining of mathematics and logic, more extreme and more abstract groups of philosophers have come. These are the logical positivists and the scholars devoted to symbolic logic. The new gospel was formulated by Ludwig Wittgenstein in his *Tractatus Logico-Philosophicus* (1922). Here the aim is precise definition and analysis in the language of science.[28] Operating in the higher levels of abstraction, logical analysis has made some significant philosophical discoveries, and aided by new machines and other technical devices it is a dominant force in the universities. To the logical positivists, a metaphysical system that cannot survive empirical testing must be abandoned. Often fiercely intolerant, these logicians have subdued rival philosophies or have caused deep schisms in those departments of philosophy that have attempted to maintain a variety and balance in the study.

In the turbulent condition of the world in this century, many of the traditional assumptions of the West have been sharply challenged. The belief in democracy as the best social order was renounced in Germany, Italy, and Russia. Progressive and liberal preconceptions were rudely shaken by the depression. The Second World War and its aftermath have reminded us of the shallowness of our civilization. As we have seen, many attempts have been made to construct a satisfactory working philosophy out of the ruins. The latest of these is existentialism, deriving from the philosophical writings of Sören Kierkegaard[29] and reinvigorated more recently by Martin Heidegger.

This doctrine abandons the hope of scientific rationality and has given up the effort to understand reality. In the hands of theologians it has been given a Christian turn, in that the existentialist accepts our human condition and constructs from life as he sees it a spiritual reality. Modern theological existentialism puts the content of faith beyond the reach of intellectual criticism. This use of the doctrine may be seen in Reinhold Niebuhr's *The Nature and Destiny of Man* (1941–1943). In other hands, such as Jean-Paul Sartre's, the conclusions to be drawn from the doctrine are very different indeed. We find ourselves in an irrational and godless world and subject to a capricious fate. In Heidegger this attitude leads to anxiety as a chronic condition of man; in Sartre it produces a permanent nausea. These ills can be met only by the courage of despair.

The faith in reason, however, is still alive, and this may be seen in the distinguished work of such scholars as Brand Blanshard, Clarence I. Lewis, Arthur E. Murphy, and Max Black.[30] These philosophers attempt with considerable success to restore reason and value to their central importance in philosophical thinking after the devastating inroads made upon the subject by excessive idealism, materialism, and skepticism during the century.

If we stand apart now from the detailed development in the separate areas and disciplines, we may see the larger features of American higher education in truer proportions. Perhaps the fact first in importance is that in these years America has come of age and is now an equal partner with Europe in learning and research. We are training our own scholars and scientists. It is true that most of the seminal ideas in the broad areas of knowledge still come from Europe or men trained in Europe; but this is less so than it was, and usually it has been America that developed and applied those ideas. A second notable feature is the increase and fragmentation of knowledge in almost every conventional field, the enormous proliferation of special studies, and the consequent demand for specialists of every kind. But perhaps of more significance than all else is the fact that we are living in an age in which science pervades and dominates all thought, in which the methods and substance of science have drawn other fields of knowledge after it, as if by the force of gravity. Certainly the remarkable prophecy of Henry Adams in 1909, that the future of thought lay in the hands of the mathematical physicists, has come to pass.[31]

With these major characteristics in mind, a number of other developments may be observed. To fill the vacuum left by the decline of the classical disciplines, and as a recognition of our own importance as a nation in the modern world, a strong movement towards the study of American history and literature has flourished in recent decades. Moreover, learning in this country has taken firm control of ideas that may have originated in Europe and has developed them into native movements, as we have seen in such elaborations in literary studies as new criticism, in the social sciences as behavioral science, and in the natural sciences as applied science. Associated with this firm control is the American tendency to put knowledge to use, a major tenet in the peculiarly native philosophy of pragmatism. The willingness of American scholars to experiment and invent is shown in the emergence of studies that reach across conventional disciplines. This may be seen in area studies, which draw upon language and literature, history, anthropology and sociology, and sometimes religion and philosophy; or in the development of comparative literature or such combinations in the sciences as biophysics and biochemistry. Related to this is the trend towards team research, especially in the sciences. This trend, however, should not blind us to the importance of the single directing mind of the scientist or scholar in the project. As an answer to intense specialization, too, such combinations as medieval studies and American studies have flourished. It is in new combinations, such as molecular biology, that the most spectacular advances will be made in the future.

The historical events that have formed the character of the United States in this century—the growing complexity of industry, society, and government, the two world wars, the depression—have had the effect of making the universities a national resource in supplying educated and trained men and in conducting research for the purposes of defense, health, and welfare. Partly in response to this fact, and partly because of the vast increase in wealth and opportunity, the number of adequate graduate schools has multiplied many times, and so of course has the number of students in them. In 1910 there may have been a dozen moderately adequate graduate schools of arts and sciences; in 1960 there were probably fifty that might be called adequate, and half of these were far above adequacy. In the decade between 1898 and 1909, approximately 3,000 doctor's degrees were awarded by all American graduate schools; in 1963 alone, the figure was about 12,000. Proportionately, it is the rising social sciences that have been the gainers, and the humanities the losers. The natural sciences, maintaining their position proportionately, have greatly increased in numbers. Even so, the quantity of scientists, engineers, and scholars to supply the needs of the country is far less than the demand. This remains true in spite of the strenuous efforts of the national government to change the condition.

A final comment may be made on the geographical and institutional distribution of learning in the country. In most general terms it may be said that the older private universities of the East have retained their eminence in humanistic studies; the universities of the Midwest are strong in the social sciences; and in the Far West the institutions have shown special strength in the natural sciences. But no region has a monopoly on any branch of knowledge, for strong departments may be found in universities in any part of the country—and this is slowly becoming as true of the South as of any other section. One thing seems to be increasingly clear: there is talent in every part of the nation. It is equally clear that there will be improvement in facilities, an increase in numbers of students, and expansion of university studies. Yet these developments alone will not guarantee the greatness of our universities.

CHAPTER VI | THE FEDERAL GOVERNMENT
AND HIGHER EDUCATION

Among the powers and functions allotted by the Constitution to the federal government and to the states, education is not mentioned.[1] It was assumed therefore, and implied by the Tenth Amendment, that education in all its phases and levels was the responsibility of each state; and this assumption persists to the present, with a very few exceptions, in spite of the profound involvement of the federal government with the colleges and universities of the country in recent decades. The states of the stripling nation, however, were slow to take on the burden of higher education, in part probably because of the number and strength of the private colleges that had been established on the eastern seaboard and partly also because of an unwillingness to offend the denominational groups that had sponsored colleges. Nevertheless, both Washington and Jefferson dreamed of founding a national university. In a message to Congress on December 2, 1806, Jefferson said:

Education is here placed among the articles of public care, not that it would be proposed to take its ordinary branches out of the hands of private enterprise, which manages so much better all the concerns to which it is equal; but a public institution can alone supply those sciences which, though rarely called for, are yet necessary to complete the circle, all the parts of which contribute to the improvement of the country, and some of them to its preservation.

One must admire the prescience of Jefferson, but the country in its youth was fearful of centralization in any form and the national university was never created. Almost at once, however, the necessity for specially trained personnel for service in the federal government became apparent, and in 1802 the Military Academy at West Point was established. In the light of history one is tempted to read a symbolic significance into the fact that the first federal institution of higher education to be founded was devoted to defense. With the wisdom granted by history, too, one may observe that the government, in establishing the Military Academy, engaged in higher education for its own practical purposes and not because of any interest in higher education as such.

The failure of the federal government and the tardiness of the states to assume control of higher education notwithstanding, there was a strong desire on the part of the public in the late eighteenth century to gain such control. This trend may be seen in the gradual secularization of the boards of trustees of the colleges as the colonial and state assemblies demanded representation on the boards equal to that enjoyed by the clergy.[2] The case for secular control of the boards was won in the nineteenth century, but the attempt of the State of New Hampshire to take over Dartmouth College was rebuffed by the famous decision of the Supreme Court of the United States. This significant decision, the first taken by the court in educational matters, made it clear that private institutions could not be captured by the will of the public alone, and it has served as a protection for private higher education to the present day.

As early as 1802 the federal government inaugurated a policy that was to have a long history and large consequences. On the admission of Ohio as a state in that year, the national government granted the land of two townships to endow a university in the state, and it continued that practice for each new state entering the union after 1802 except for Maine, Texas, and West Virginia. But these actions, and other scattered and occasional small grants and contracts for education, were merely the prologue to the Morrill Act of 1862 establishing the Land Grant colleges for higher education in agriculture and the mechanic arts. The purpose of the act was to encourage the states in the training of badly needed experts in industry and farming; and towards this end the Land Grant Act gave to each state for the establishment of a college 30,000 acres of land, or the equivalent in scrip, for each senator and representative in Congress. In 1890 a second Morrill Act continued the award of appropriations and loans to the states for the teaching of engineering, agriculture, and the sciences and for training students in military science. The Land Grant acts have had a notable effect on higher education in America and now support sixty-eight colleges and universities.[3] Possibly the Land Grant Act of 1862 was a recognition by the government of a limited degree of responsibility for higher education; at least the act exhibited a more generous conception of the role of higher education in the national interest. At the same time, it should be said that the federal government had its own purposes in view and made its awards from bountiful resources of land that it had recently acquired and was in no position to exploit to its own advantage. It is clear that the government's interests were in vocational and professional rather than in liberal education, in practical scientific research, and in the training of the many rather than the few. But whatever the motives, it is clear that the Land Grant acts and the associated Hatch Act of 1887, establishing experimental stations for agriculture in each of the states, have been most advantageous for the country.

The cautious attitude of the federal government towards higher education is well illustrated by the establishment of the Bureau of Education in 1867. Most European countries head up their national system of education by a post of cabinet stature. No such position was intended for the person in charge of the Bureau. In fact, the Bureau had virtually no powers, but was to be a center for collecting and disseminating useful information. And this the Office of Education has remained, though in 1958 its duties were expanded by the National Defense Education Act, as we shall see. In the meantime, various immediate necessities have impelled the government to establish such agencies as the Army Medical School in 1893 and the Army War

College in 1901. These were peripheral, of course. An action much closer to the colleges was the inauguration of the Reserve Officers Training Corps, which prepared undergraduates for military action in the First World War and utilized the facilities of many colleges during the war by its Students' Army Training Corps. This prepared the way for the later continuing ROTC programs in the colleges for the army, navy, and air force and for the huge operations of the Second World War when the government took over the facilities, and parts of the faculties, of many institutions, to train soldiers and sailors for the numerous aspects of modern warfare. Needless to say, this action of the government's saved many institutions from bankruptcy.

A step of a different kind was that taken during the depression in the 1930s in establishing the National Youth Administration to provide employment and money by which students could continue their education. As generous as this action on the part of the government was, it paled by comparison with the Servicemen's Readjustment Act of 1944, sometimes referred to as Public Law 346 and more popularly as the G. I. Bill, and its successor, Public Law 550, and the later provisions for veterans of the Korean War. The operation of these laws was immensely successful, and entirely without precedent, as three and a half million students took advantage of the provisions to obtain further education. It is not unlikely that the good experience with the G. I. Bill pointed the way to a national scholarship plan and foreshadowed the terms of such a plan. The provision of allowing the recipient of a scholarship to choose within approved limits the institution he wished to attend and the studies he wished to pursue avoided many of the obstacles to congressional legislation, such as the fear of federal control, the conflict between church and state, and the problem of segregation. Even from such a sketchy account of the relations between the government and higher education, one can see that between Jefferson's prescient statement in 1806 and the actions following the Second World War the connection had become considerably closer.

There were numerous other ties between the government and the nation's educational institutions. Faculty members of the universities and colleges were often called to Washington on advisory commissions; conferences on the state of education were frequent, the most notable of these being President Truman's Commission on Higher Education, appointed in 1946, and President Eisenhower's Committee on Education Beyond High School, in 1956. Before the Second World War and after, there was a steady increase in the number of government actions that affected directly or indirectly the institutions of higher education. One may mention such things as the sale or gift of surplus property to the colleges, loans for college housing programs, the Fulbright Act of 1946 to use the credits the government had acquired abroad, and the Smith-Mundt Act of 1948, which promoted educational exchanges with other nations. Through all these activities, however, it is not possible to see any general policy directing the operations of the federal government.

With the beginning of the Second World War, the government drew even more heavily upon the trained personnel of the universities and colleges for advice on strategy, propaganda, intelligence, or economics. For these purposes anthropologists, psychologists, historians, economists, and linguists were called upon. And, as we have seen, the campuses of the colleges and universities were widely used for training military personnel. During the war and since, however, the universities of the country, and to a much smaller extent the colleges, have been employed in a different and more critical service for the government: to conduct a number of vast programs of scientific research and development, mainly in the physical and biological sciences and engineering, but spreading in late years into several of the social sciences. In the war itself, of course, mathematicians, physicists, chemists, and engineers from the universities were drawn to such centers as the Metallurgical Laboratory at the University of Chicago, the Applied Physics Laboratory at Johns Hopkins, the Jet Propulsion Laboratory at the California Institute of Technology, and the Radiation Laboratory at the Massachusetts Institute of Technology. These institutions assembled the scientists and conducted research and development for the country's defense system. From them evolved such government centers as Los Alamos and Livermore operated by the University of California, Lincoln Laboratory at MIT, and the Brookhaven National Laboratory, operated by nine associated universities—to name only a few among some twenty-five. The astonishing success of the university scientist and engineer in developing uranium technology, the proximity fuse, rockets, and radar has made them the most vital partners of the government in national defense. In 1945 Vannevar Bush, at President Roosevelt's request, drew up a program for national scientific research, and at his suggestion the National Science Foundation was established in 1950 in what now looks like a modest program.[4] In 1940 the federal government provided $15 million in grants and contracts to universities and colleges for research and development. In 1960 the figure had grown to $462 million and is increasing with each year. In a few of the universities most active in federal research and development, government funds form as much as a quarter of the institution's annual income. The statement of Abraham A. Ribicoff, then Secretary of Health, Education and Welfare, to a committee of the House of Representatives in March 1961, was sober fact:

the question of whether the Federal Government should play a part in the enterprise of higher education is simply not a real one. The Federal Government has had an important part in that enterprise for 100 years. Its part has grown dramatically in the last 20 years, and the real question that faces us . . . is what shall the Federal Government do now, in 1961, to play its part in ways that will contribute to the continued development of a strong and vital system of higher education.[5]

The country, and its legislators, came only slowly to share Ribicoff's position. It was clear, of course, that university scientists and engineers in government laboratories had hastened the winning of the war. For the physical sciences that were mainly responsible for this, heavy and continuing financial support was provided. In 1958 it was estimated that 44 percent of the federal monies spent for research was allotted to the physical sciences, and an additional 29 percent was spent in engineering.[6] In dollar amounts, too, the increase was immense as America met the challenges of the Soviet government in Korea and later in the launching of sputnik. Obviously, the first priority was the defense of the nation. By 1960 the government's total expenditures for research and development had reached the enormous figure of $7.7 billion, of which $760 million were spent in universities and colleges. This larger total, however, included aspects other than the physical sciences. In 1960 the sum of $400 million was appropriated for the National Institutes of Health, more than $100 million above the budgeted request and more than $300 million above the appropriation of 1955. Though it has been estimated that as many as eighty federal agencies deal with the colleges and universities in awarding research and development projects, making loans, and granting fellowships and scholarships, the principal government agencies serving as sponsors of research between 1955 and 1960 were seven in number. The table listed here shows the agency and the percentage of research funds provided by each.[7]

Agency	Percentage of research funds
Department of Defense	39.8
Public Health Service	30.0
National Science Foundation	11.1
Atomic Energy Commission	8.0
Department of Agriculture	6.0
National Aeronautics and Space Agency	2.6
Office of Education	2.0

From this table it may be seen that the primary emphasis during these years of the cold war was put upon the military security of the country, and that the sciences in the universities and colleges chiefly engaged in research are the physical sciences. This emphasis would be even more clearly seen if the figures for development employing engineers and technologists were added. The government's interest in the public health of the nation was a long-standing one but, as we have seen, the research appropriations bestowed on the National Institutes of Health between 1955 and 1960 were greatly augmented. Moreover, as the country assumed the vast responsibilities of leadership after the Second World War, large sums were appropriated for such related purposes as development programs in other countries, specialized training and education, advisory experts on government programs, educational services for foreign visitors, fellowships and scholarships. In all these programs the faculty people of the universities and colleges were deeply involved. It may be added that the many agencies have dealt with the institutions and the individuals according to their need. The agency awards contracts and grants to centers, to institutions, to professors, or to students as its purpose is served, though no unrestricted assistance is given to institutions of higher education. It is noticeable that federal programs emphasize research and graduate education.

From all the operations of the government, no coordinating agency and no coordinating policy towards the universities and colleges have evolved. The federal interest has grown over the years and remains a patchwork. When the National Science Foundation was established in 1950, there was some idea of centralizing the operations of the government in "mathematical, physical, medical, biological, engineering, and other sciences" under its control and of developing a rational policy for the promotion, evaluation, and correlation of research in these fields. Little progress was made towards this end. The launching of the first sputnik, however, caused the President's Science Advisory Committee to recommend the establishment of a Federal Council on Science and Technology, composed of representatives of the important science programs, in the hope that a policy in these activities would be a result. One fruitful recommendation of the council was that the close connection between research and graduate education should be emphasized, and this suggestion had a strong effect on the

National Defense Education Act of 1958, which provided funds for fellowships and scholarships to strengthen scientific education, and funds to create and support new graduate programs. Still, it is easy to agree with Charles Kidd's assertion that "the federal government as a whole has had only very vague research policies and objectives. What the federal government is trying to do is simply the sum of the objectives of the various agencies."[8] These comments refer mainly to research for military defense and health. But when the urgencies of the cold war brought in a large new dimension of the government's interest—American foreign policy—with the demand for trained manpower that only the universities and the colleges could produce, the government's relation to educational institutions was not changed. In his speech to the Senate on June 27, 1961, Senator Fulbright said that the country had "no solid legislative base which makes it clear that these programs are an essential part of our foreign relations." To fill this vacuum, the International Cooperation Adminstration expanded its operations to award contracts to American universities and colleges for the purpose of assisting foreign countries to develop their own educational institutions. The Act for International Development in 1961 aimed to provide technical assistance to foreign countries in the fields of education, health, economics, and housing, and the exchange programs that have come from this act have been of much interest and advantage to higher education, both in America and abroad. But however excellent these many programs are, they do not simplify the relationship between the government and higher education.

Before 1958 it is clear that the federal government had not assumed a heavy obligation towards the support and improvement of higher education. Indeed, in employing the services of the universities and the colleges for its own purposes and needs, the government may be said to have had a narrow, and perhaps ungenerous, conception of the proper relation between them. The passage of the National Defense Education Act in 1958, however, was a change of direction in the thinking of Congress that may be significant. In Title I of the act,

Congress declared that "the security of the Nation requires the fullest development of the mental resources and technical skills of its young men and women," and further, "This requires programs that will give assurance that no student of ability will be denied an opportunity for higher education because of financial need." This was to see the national interest in larger terms than before. To implement the new policy, a program of student loans and graduate fellowships was inaugurated in all fields of study, and in 1959 nearly 10,000 awards of all kinds were made. The terms of the loans were generous, both to the individuals and to their institutions. This was a long step towards the ultimate establishment of a national scholarship plan. Such a plan had no real precedent; the G. I. Bills of 1944 and 1952 were enacted for very different reasons. The Graduate Fellowship Program was drastically new in that it allowed fellowships in all fields of study. By 1961, under this part of the NDEA 4,000 fellowships had been awarded: 26 percent went to students in the humanities, 6 percent in education, 29 percent in the social sciences, 12 percent in the biological sciences, 19 percent in the physical sciences, and 8 percent in engineering.[9] The general drift towards a more liberal treatment of higher education is possibly confirmed by the more recent act of Congress, signed by President Johnson on December 16, 1963, allotting $1.2 billion over a three-year period to aid the colleges by loans to provide better facilities, libraries, laboratories, and dormitories. Perhaps a corner has been turned, but it would probably be premature to think that the government and higher education regard themselves as eager collaborators in a venture important to both sides.[10]

In the autumn of 1964 Congress passed the National Defense Education Act (Extension and Amendments). By the provisions of this later bill, the sum of $1.8 billion was added for loans in the next three years to provide further for better facilities, libraries, laboratories, and dormitories; and the grants to institutions and the loans to students were made more generous. Furthermore, the area of the government's interest in specific subjects was slightly expanded.

In sum, then, we see that the National Defense Education Acts may be the beginning of a real governmental policy concerning its relations with higher education. If that is saying too much, it can be said nevertheless that, by increasing massively the facilities and support for graduate education, the government has assumed an obligation for higher education well beyond any earlier venture. To be sure, this is not done in the interest of education as such. The motives of Congress in establishing new graduate schools, in encouraging old graduate schools to add new programs, and in providing graduate fellowships were undoubtedly of several kinds. There was the genuine desire to increase the opportunities for higher study for individuals; there was the intention to provide a wider range of graduate schools in more areas of the country; and there was undoubtedly the hope on the part of the members of Congress of ingratiating themselves with their constituents. Probably many lawmakers were surprised and offended when there was not greater acclaim in some quarters for the sudden expansion of the numbers of graduate schools. The older graduate schools felt that the quality of education was threatened as they sometimes lost scarce talent to the new schools. In any case, by the passage of the NDEA a beginning had been made towards a government policy as the effort to train the nation's manpower in new institutions and specific fields took the positive step towards the education of teachers for the schools and colleges in mathematics, the sciences, and the languages.

The most immediately effective part of the NDEA operation was the student loan program. By 1959 more than 1,400 of the nation's 2,000 colleges were participating in it. The program of loans to institutions for construction of nonacademic facilities was also popular, involving about 600 institutions. Less than half that number obtained loans or grants for the construction of research facilities. But it was probably disturbing to Congress that not more than 100 universities in the country were deeply involved in the research programs of the government. Moreover, of the 100, in almost every list 25 universities appear as recipients of the bulk of federal money for research, the largest grants for facilities and equipment and for education and training. Of the most favored institutions, 16 received more than $10 million; 7 more than $20 million; and 4 more than $50 million. In 1960, universities and colleges received in all about $800 million from the government for research and development.[11] Inevitably, too, the 25 strongest universities attracted the best of the students on the graduate fellowships provided by the government programs. It was mainly to rectify the narrow base in research and specialized education that Congress passed the NDEA program. The strength of major institutions of higher education, however, is of long standing, and the situation will not soon be altered.

From the foregoing we may see the present deep involvement of the country's institutions of higher education in the federal government's programs for research, development, and the training of specialized personnel. The resources of the colleges and universities are heavily strained to support the great number and variety of federal activities:[12] the operation of government-owned research centers, such as Los Alamos or Brookhaven; the performance of basic research in the universities; the provision of specialized educational and training programs; the operation of educational assistance and development programs in foreign countries; the training of federal employees, both civilian and military, at home and abroad; advisory service by faculty experts on government programs; and the provision of educational services for faculty and students from abroad, and other foreign visitors, in support of United States foreign policy. Most of this activity began during the Second World War; the chief and obvious fact about the developments of the last quarter century is that the government has come to rely heavily upon the institutions of higher education for scientific research, engineering technology, and trained manpower for the purposes of defense, health, and operating procedures.

This reliance is new to the universities and colleges and has materially altered the nature and function of those institutions most active in federal programs. For this reason it is especially important for the institutions of higher learning to comprehend the characteristics of the government's many programs, and the first point to observe is that there is no coordinating body among the government's agencies and no consistent body of practice that may as yet be called a policy. Each agency, as we have seen, deals with research and development centers, institutions, projects, faculty members, and students for its own needs and in its own fashion. In the nineteenth century the government had mainly conducted its research and development in its own institutions and laboratories. Its association with higher education came primarily from its interest in public lands, farmers, and industrial technicians. It characteristically emphasized vocational and professional rather than liberal education. Such research as the government engaged in was "mission-directed" and immediately practical. Insofar as the federal government was concerned with education, it was for the multitude rather than the few.

Many of these characteristics have lingered into the present day. There seems very little more coordination in the government's practices than formerly, but a beginning may have been made. As before, too, the federal involvement in higher education is for its own purposes and not for the benefit of education as a whole. Accordingly, the federal government in the critical times of the Second World War and the cold war has not only vastly increased its practical research programs in the physical, biological, and medical sciences, but has sharpened its interest in special subjects there and in many other areas. An example of this may be seen in its engagement in international education in connection with foreign policy. As before, the government is primarily interested in the results of practical research and the development of weapons, instruments, and ideas for immediate use, and this may be seen in the fact that only 7 percent of the money expended in the universities is awarded for basic research. Also as we have seen, the government's activities are highly concentrated in the relatively few institutions that have the facilities and personnel to conduct the research and the training programs. Another characteristic is that the public and private institutions actively engaged in these projects are almost equal in number.

The cumulative effect of the government's involvement in higher education in the last twenty years has been to create a feeling that the federal government may one day assume the full responsibility for higher education in America. Because of the restraint of the government agencies, the educational institutions have almost entirely lost their fear of an imposed government control. But the public has not progressed so fast, and Congress is responsive to the public. To overcome such fears a number of ingenious devices would have to be employed and new formulas invented if a head-on conflict with such deeply felt principles as the separation of church and state is to be evaded. It is to be hoped that the integrity of the colleges and universities can be maintained, but one's sense of the inevitability of history is not lessened by the succession of presidential commissions in recent years—the President's Commission on Higher Education of 1946, the Hoover Commission of 1947, and the President's Committee of 1956. Each of these bodies has shown a strong desire for a coherent set of government policies dealing with higher education, and some progress has been made. The 1956 committee under the chairmanship of Devereux C. Josephs had considerable effect upon governmental legislation: the National Defense Education Act was in part a product of its recommendations. The panel of the President's Science Advisory Committee under Glenn T. Seaborg in its report of 1960 further emphasized the close relation between government-supported research in the universities and graduate education, and urged the government to seek forms of support that would permit the universities to enlarge their permanent facilities.

The activities of the government in higher education are scattered among many federal agencies; and the universities and colleges on their side have developed no single agency to speak for higher education. The American Council on Education is perhaps in the best position to do this, but seldom does so to the general satisfaction of the universities and colleges. Other organizations represent particular sections of higher education, such as the American Association for the Advancement of Science, the Social Science Research Council, and the American Council of Learned Societies. At a less general level there are such organizations as the Association of American Universities, the Association of American Colleges, the Association of Land Grant Colleges and State Universities, and the National Association of State Universities, besides many other groups united by denominational or similar bonds. At still another level are organizations whose membership is made up of people tied together by reason of their professional interests, such as the Modern Language Association, the American Historical Association, the American Chemical Society, or the American Association of University Professors. The first three of these seem to be in the process of sharpening specialization and further fragmentation. Occasionally under pressure the universities combine to do a job the government wants done, as in the laboratory center at Brookhaven. But in general each institution of higher education speaks for itself and deals with the particular government agency directly. Both the universities and the government seem to prefer this piecemeal arrangement. When one organization did make its wishes known, it was to take a self-regarding and parochial position: Chancellor John T. Caldwell, in speaking for the Association of Land Grant Colleges and State Universities, urged that federal aid "be expended *only* in institutions established, supported and controlled through the constitutional organs of civil government."[13] Clear-cut as this suggestion was in its confrontation of the vexed issue of church and state, it would have been scientifically and politically disastrous for Congress to adopt it. Equally disastrous would have been the adoption of a proposal that only independent institutions should deal with the federal government.

This leads us to consider further the point of view of the universities and colleges themselves.[14] What is the impact on the system of higher education as a whole, as well as the internal effect upon the single institution? Often, but not always, the effect will be identical. Special care must be used to gauge the effects of federal programs on the quality and nature of higher education; to a great extent, but not always, the government's interest is more quantitative than that of the universities and colleges.

In considering the impact of federal activity on higher education across the nation, one must say that it has been generally good, though varied and uneven. In the area of scientific research especially, higher education has felt a quickening spirit, and a new vigor has permeated the whole system, clear down to the freshman in college. In the colleges and universities the research activities and functions have been greatly expanded, and a sense of public service has been wakened. There are deficits as well as assets, of course, where the scientific method has been applied inappropriately or where science has shouldered out other useful studies. And there are, inevitably, some areas in which government programs have had little effect. One of the most serious effects of federal activity has been the concentration of funds in a relatively few universities, those capable in terms of facilities and manpower of performing the services required by the government. Thus, the gaps have inevitably widened between the strong and the weak institutions, between the colleges and the graduate schools, between the sciences (and a few social sciences) that are aided by federal funds and the humanities that have none.[15] In a handful of the most active universities, government contracts and grants for research are being built into the annual budgets; a sudden withdrawal of funds would be as disastrous as real peace would be to industry. And following the concentration of funds there is an equal concentration of talent in scientists and students. Moreover, the cost of modern scientific research, utilizing such instruments as cyclotrons, accelerators, and computers, to say nothing of increased physical plant and manpower, has grown so great that no university has sufficient resources of its own. The institutions must rely upon the government for support. And, as I have said, the concentration of the government's demand for research and development in the physical sciences, the biological sciences, and engineering has the effect of narrowing the programs of basic research in the universities. Other difficulties caused by government programs may be mentioned briefly: the sharpened rivalries among universities for eminent specialists as the institutions use federal funds to attract scarce scientists and scholars from other universities with similar programs; or the professors bargaining in the academic market place for larger salaries and lighter teaching loads, and offering to bring to a new institution a handsome government contract.

These are some of the effects of federal activity in the educational system at large. There are others that may come home more sharply to the individual institution, but these too are often national in their operation. One is the tendency for some professors to become more attached to the special federal research they are working on than to their home institution and its purposes. Another is the absence of the faculty member from the campus on a mission for the government. Still another is the split in the faculty between those who have a federal contract or are at work on a government project and those who have nothing but their regular salaries. This almost invariably leads to a disparity in salaries, since the man on a federal contract will add two ninths of his salary to his income for summer work. The institution heavily engaged in government programs is usually left with many major problems, such as the imbalance in salaries, terms of tenure, and the division between the college and the graduate school. Perhaps the most serious of these problems, and possibly the most common, is the deterioration of teaching, especially in the colleges. The independent small college has difficulty in recruiting and maintaining a competent faculty in many fields, and in the university college the teaching of undergraduates is increasingly done by graduate assistants and often by those who cannot obtain handsome fellowships.

One other comment in this context deserves a special paragraph. The ambition, poor judgment, or greediness of universities has sometimes led them to take on federal programs for which they have no special talents. The government agencies have often shown a remarkable restraint in refusing to interfere with the freedom of research, but a young scientist often shows less when tempted to sacrifice his own freedom by attaching himself to the lucrative contract of an older man. Further, the university and the professor are often seduced into accepting from a government agency a contract that does not have the highest priority of either. The government, eager to get a certain job done, will take what it can get, but it will seldom or never exercise direct control. The following statement by Richard G. Axt is a fair comment on this matter:

No evidence has been found for the existence of direct controls by the Federal Government, or any of its agencies, over either public or private higher education or for the desire for such controls. What does exist is an influence over the program and policies of higher education resulting from the many separate, uncoordinated federal programs in higher education, each of which emphasizes the interests of the federal department or agency sponsoring it rather than the general needs of higher education.[16]

It is true that in "some circumstances seduction may be a crime, but it is quite a different crime from rape."[17] The only preservative of integrity is for the institution and the professor to say "no." It is most important to keep in mind the distinction between the purposes and priorities of the government and those of the institution. A clear understanding of the rights and limitations on each side would have spared the nation the acrimonious debates of the McCarthy era and many buffetings of conscience.

Beyond these larger questions, there are other points of friction between the government agencies and the institutions. As I have said above, the fear of government control in any direct sense has largely evaporated, even in the private institutions, and this is a tribute to federal restraint. The disturbance of individual loyalties is more intangible and lingering, but that is a problem for colleges and universities that antedates the Second World War. There are, however, smaller and more annoying points of trouble. One that disturbs the institutions and the government, rather than the scientist doing a job for the government, is the matter of overhead. The institutions frequently feel that Congress is niggardly in allowing no more than the usual 15 percent, which is altogether inadequate to pay the costs for management, facilities, and other necessities, and that the government is inclined to drive a hard bargain rather than to treat higher education as a companion in good work for the nation. In any case, the payments to the institutions from the federal agencies are sometimes unconscionably delayed and the college or university suffers undue hardship. The scientist who does the research often feels that such overhead as the government allows ought to come to him rather than to his institution. The scientist is also impatient of the proposals and reports of progress upon his project, which he has to prepare at great expense of time; but this feeling may be countered by reminding him that no one is forcing him to undertake the project and that some projects are manufactured for the sake of prestige.

More serious from the point of view of the institutions and the scientist is the governmental demand for secrecy and for padlocked security. Secrecy runs directly contrary in principle to one of the fundamental functions of the universities and colleges, one of whose major obligations as educational institutions is to disseminate knowledge. In the matter of security the suspicious demand of Congress that all personnel participating in the National Defense Education Act take a loyalty oath and subscribe to an affidavit as well as an affront to the individual's integrity and put an impossible burden upon the institution at the same time. Fortunately this demand has yielded to protest, but one cannot be sure that Congress understood or sympathized with the complaint of the institutions and the individuals. One last important criticism of the federal programs may be made from the point of view of the institutions of higher learning. This is the unevenness of the government's patronage, which neglects the humanities and most of the social sciences, and in some of the sciences, for example the medical ones, grants more funds than the institutions can use. Moreover, the proportion of research monies allowed to basic research, as opposed to immediate project and developmental allocations, is contrary to the essential purpose of the university. But here again one might answer that a knowledge of the history of the operations of the government in higher education should have warned the individual and his institution that he could expect nothing else. The government's neglect of the areas of opinion and taste that are the province of the social sciences and humanities may be a blessing in disguise.

If these comments have seemed too exclusively centered on the point of view of higher education, a few further observations may do something to restore the balance. The events of history and the necessities of the present have put the nation at an impasse. On one side, we strongly hold to old principles and traditions—the separation of church and state, the public fear of federal control, and our more recent stand against segregation. On the other side, we have arrived at the conviction that higher education provides essential services for the nation; and to perform these services we need to engage the efforts of all the present institutions and to create new ones as well. In the past the government met its necessities by a series of expedient, tentative, and uncoordinated actions, improvised to meet the occasion of the moment, and had developed no comprehensive policy. But the operations of the Second World War convinced the government that science and trained manpower were by far the most precious of the nation's resources, and the adoption of Vannevar Bush's proposals in his report, *Science, the Endless Frontier,* established research and development, including the training of specialists, as the major concern of the federal government. It is clear that new formulas, ingeniously employed, will have to be used if we are to bring the whole of higher education into the service of the nation. The government is in higher education to stay, and only such great resources as it possesses will be adequate for modern scientific research.

On the other hand, the universities and the colleges can conduct that research best, and only they can produce the necessary trained manpower. In this situation it is to be hoped that higher education will remember its other duties—to advance basic knowledge in all fields of learning and to teach the young who will be the leaders of the country in all fields.

So far, of course, no comprehensive and consistent policy in dealing with higher education has been formulated by the government, and perhaps none should be. But what would be of much value to both sides would be an improved bureau for information rather than control. Such an office could keep all the agencies of the federal government and all the institutions of higher education informed about current operations and practices much more adequately than they are at present; it could undertake many kinds of studies that would be useful in appraising trends in educational policy and practice and in foreseeing problems. Such a bureau should be operated by a much strengthened Office of Education in Health, Education and Welfare. And this bureau should concentrate much more than it does now on the affairs and condition of higher education. On the part of higher education, there is an equal need for an organization of a comprehensive capacity and high quality to present to the government the point of view of the universities and colleges, to formulate such policy as seems wise, and to assure integrity, independence, and excellence. It is to be hoped that, if such a committee is ever set up, its members will be chosen for their competence rather than for their political significance. Until better plans are in effect, and more illuminating information is available, it is best for the institutions of higher education to be aware of their own traditional purposes and to be courageous in defense of them.

CHAPTER VII | AMERICAN
HIGHER EDUCATION TODAY

Crisis is the chronic condition of higher education in our dynamic democracy, and today, almost twenty years after the end of the Second World War, events again seem to be moving towards a point where not only adjustments but drastic decisions will have to be made. Ironically, this new period of crisis comes upon us when the United States has become a leader in world education. Scholars and students come to us from many parts of the world at a time when our educational establishment is in disorder and has lost, as a whole, any clear sense of direction. They come for our scientific knowledge and engineering techniques, and often give us little credit for any culture or learning beyond these areas. In so thinking, they are abetted by the prevailing temper of the American public, which is still essentially optimistic, pragmatic, and utilitarian in spite of the demonstrable shortcomings of that point of view.

But wiser heads in the academic profession, among the public, and in the government are deeply concerned about the present state of higher education. This may be seen in the numerous commissions and committees, many of them federal, which have addressed themselves to the plight of higher education since the end of the war. The most obvious reason for concern has been quantitative. Since the G. I. Bill of Rights sent almost five million veterans back to continue their education, the flood of students to the colleges and universities has never slackened, and it is predicted that the number of students will be twice as great by 1975.

A second matter that has concerned higher education in recent years has been the nature and extent of the demands of the federal government upon the universities and colleges for research on the problems of national defense and health. These demands have fallen heavily upon the science faculties of the hundred universities that are deeply involved in research sponsored by the government. The impact has been far-reaching, and both beneficial and detrimental. In the individual university, research facilities for the sciences have been improved and the faculty augmented. But the balance in the institution has often been upset as the graduate school that trained the specialists and conducted the research became disproportionately important compared to the college, and as the scientist was more favored than his colleagues in the humanities and the social sciences. For the educational establishment as a whole, the benefits and detriments were likewise balanced. The intellectual life of higher education was quickened, but the concentration of government grants favored the already strong institutions. A deeper cause of concern was that only 7 percent of the massive support the government granted to the colleges and universities was for basic research, and the remainder was awarded for immediate, developmental research towards a designated end. The major question now is whether in this imbalance the universities can regain control of their own purposes and future.

A third point of concern at the present time is the question of the place and function of the college in the total educational plan—a question that does not rise directly from government demand, but is a consequence of international forces and events since the release of atomic energy, Soviet truculence, and Soviet scientific advances. This is more particularly a problem for the college and will be discussed in some detail below; but the question of the future of the college has implications for the whole form and fabric of higher education in this country.

The patterns of collegiate education that we have seen developing earlier in the century, as answers to the chaos caused by the explosion of knowledge and the elective system, have become somewhat stabilized, and experiment has been less bold in recent years. The system of group requirements for distribution and a major field for concentration, with a comprehensive examination in the major, has been very widely adopted. The emphasis upon honors work begun by Swarthmore forty years ago has increased until almost every respectable college requires a rigorous examination in the field of the major and formidable independent work of an increasingly high quality, for an honors degree. Outside examiners are used more often and the volume of excellent work has been greatly increased, but there has been little further refinement in methods since World War II. The strong trend towards greater specialization in the later college years and the invasion of college studies by the substance and techniques of the graduate schools has made the colleges uneasy about the major, and it has suggested to some educators the advisability of broadening the major field into an interdisciplinary program of concentration comparable to the Modern Greats of Oxford.[1] This would better prepare the student who is going on to graduate or professional training and would provide a richer experience for the student who accepts the bachelor's degree as terminal. Such a move will encounter the vested interests of the departments, however, and progress will be slow.

The progressive movement that informed the curriculums of such colleges as Antioch, Sarah Lawrence, and Bennington has not made many converts.[2] But its technique of developing the interest of the student and combining academic work with experience in the world has been widely adopted in the plans of conventional colleges; this often takes the form of a senior essay or project. The great success of such a device lies in the fact that the student is actively engaged in his own education and has something that is peculiarly his own. Such ventures often illustrate by their therapeutic and tangible results the point that the faculties hitherto have not been demanding enough of their undergraduates.

There has also been dissatisfaction, almost from the beginning, with the system of group requirements for distribution. It was felt that a core of the most important subjects should make up this part of the student's program. The purpose of such courses was to acquaint the student, in the limited time allowed, with the intellectual and spiritual tradition of the Western world. This was general education as Columbia and later Chicago imagined it, thereby inaugurating an important movement in collegiate education.[3] The program at St. John's in Annapolis represents an extreme, with special content and methods. The Harvard plan promulgated in the booklet, *General Education in a Free Society* (1945), rose from the same fears of the fragmentation of knowledge and from the same aims that provided the impetus for the Columbia plan, but is actually different. General education has flourished for four decades and has been perhaps the most serious effort in this century to recapture the integrity of a liberal education. But recently general education has been challenged on the one hand by the rival movement of advanced credit and advanced standing, which has made a common educational experience for all students impossible, and on the other by the demand of the students for early specialization—a demand encouraged by the graduate and professional schools that they hope to enter. Most colleges with programs of general education are now in the process of reappraising their curriculums, and some will abandon the idea. Harvard, the most recent of the powerful proponents of general education, is making such a reappraisal and will probably continue its program after taking into account the new developments since 1945.

From these several elements, then, the American college has so far shaped its course. And the result may be viewed with a great deal of pride, though with little complacency. In the quality of its performance, the American college has drawn up appreciably upon the institutions of continental Europe and also upon Oxford and Cambridge. The statement of the German universities in 1905, that they would regard the American bachelor's degree as only the equivalent of a leaving certificate from the Gymnasium, and then only if the degree was awarded by an institution that was a member of the

Association of American Universities, is completely out of date today. In every part of our country there now exist numbers of excellent small colleges—the men's and women's colleges of New England and New York, the group of distinguished colleges about Philadelphia, colleges in Virginia and further south, in Ohio and Indiana, in the further Middle West, and on the Pacific coast, both north and south. In these institutions the traditions of great teaching and sound learning flourish. Nor has that tradition been forgotten in many of our great universities, however deep they may be in service for the state and federal government. But if the colleges are to remain true to their traditions, they must be prepared to change with the changing times and to make their education relevant while keeping it liberal.

Recent trends, then, have raised many questions concerning the form and content of the traditional college of liberal arts. The normal four-year span of the college program, which probably rose from the inadequacy of elementary and secondary education in colonial days, is not sacrosanct, and the length of the period has been challenged often in the past. In the nineteenth century the bachelor's degree often required only three years; this was true at Johns Hopkins, Harvard, and Yale, among others. In the present state of affairs, however, a new argument has been added to the challenge. Not only does the success of the advanced-standing movement threaten to shorten the traditional length of the college course, but the strong trend towards early specialization in pre-professional courses in the programs of the upper years threatens to drive out the liberal studies that make for perspective and maturity. Between the two pressures, the traditional college of liberal arts in this country may be drastically altered, for both pressures make towards acceleration, and the time saved will inevitably be at the cost of the liberal studies.[4]

The effect of the advanced-placement and advanced-standing movement has already been considerable and promises to be greater in the future. At Harvard, for example, approximately 150 students are admitted to the sophomore class directly from secondary school;

and many other substantial colleges of the country are making comparable adjustments. One may fairly say that it is high time that the nation's secondary schools relieved the colleges of several elementary studies, and in this category one may mention English composition, calculus, and a firm control of at least one modern foreign language. But questions come from both directions: Are the high schools the country over capable of doing an adequate job in these studies and in some equally important liberal studies, such as history or literature? And next, if the high schools should prove capable, or a substantial proportion of them should, what will the colleges do with the time saved? At present, the students allowed to graduate in three years have for the most part not taken advantage of the opportunity, but have stayed in the universities an additional year for the sake of enriching their educational experience. This is evidence of great national wealth and a spirit of leisure; but what will happen if hard times come upon us again, or what will happen in the small college whose resources will be unequal to carrying the advanced student as far as he wishes to go?

Quite beyond the program of studies in college, a further question presents itself. If the form of the college is appreciably changed, what will happen to the elaborate, and to many people precious, collegiate way of life that has been so assiduously fostered in the last one hundred years? The countries of continental Europe have never seen the need of such an extended process of maturing as our students have enjoyed. They have been content with the educational procedure that takes the student from the Gymnasium or the lycée directly to his professional training in the university. Yet, without being too fond of the romantic glamor of college life in America, one may ask whether the French, German, or Soviet student is not lacking in some aspects of his full maturity because of the purely intellectual emphasis that European education imposes. In any case, drastic change in the form of the college throughout the country will be slow in coming, partly because of the affection the country has for its colleges and partly because the high schools in many areas will not be capable of the excellent teaching that advanced placement should require. In the meanwhile, the colleges should do some hard thinking about their place in the country's educational establishment.

In the upper years of the college, as I have said, the pressure is quite as great and equally subversive of the liberal ideal as the student, abetted by his professionalized teacher, presses towards the graduate or professional school. The fact is that now more than 75 percent of the graduates of the best colleges of the East go on to advanced work. The bachelor's degree is no longer terminal, and the college is, as it has been called, a "waiting room" for the upper schools. The victims of this trend, as I have suggested, are the liberal studies, which do not visibly guarantee entrance to medical, law, or graduate school, though they may provide the most valuable educational experience the student can gain for living with himself and his society. It would be well here if the colleges would rethink their traditional programs in the field of concentration in order to provide a broader, richer, and more liberal base upon which a future structure of specialization may be erected. There would be the additional advantage, moreover, of offering a better education to those students for whom the bachelor's degree is terminal.

We should not delude ourselves that reforms running counter to the intensely departmental structure of our universities and colleges will easily be achieved. The universities, and to a much lesser extent the colleges, are staffed wth teachers who think that their primary obligation is the advancement of knowledge. This undoubtedly is a major function of the university. But it is now widely recognized that in many colleges the function of teaching has deteriorated. The reasons are not far to seek. If the distinguished scientist or scholar can find time at all from his life of research to teach undergraduates, he is likely to consider them as future scholars in his own field. If he is teaching freshmen, the course will probably be taught as if it were the first course on the long journey towards the doctor's degree in that discipline. The young teacher just out of graduate school, still hypnotized by the intense specialization demanded by that experience, is likely to be even narrower and more professional than his master. As Robert Hutchins wryly remarked, "It is hardly an exaggeration to say that university departments exist to train people to teach in university departments." What usually happens in undergraduate classes today is that while the professor, trained in the spirit of science to be objective and neutral, gives the lectures, such personal teaching as is done is in the hands of graduate students who may or may not be instinctively good teachers, but who are usually lacking in experience. If the student's program is made up entirely of such courses, we should not be surprised if the light of learning flickers and is soon extinguished. This is the state of teaching in many university colleges; in the small independent colleges only some of the same problems exist, but there is the added difficulty that it is frequently impossible for such colleges to recruit and retain a competent and well-trained faculty.

The undergraduate of the sixth and seventh decades of the twentieth century is a much more serious person than his precedessor of forty years ago. If he is the son of a graduate of the college, he is probably not innately abler than his father, but he is better motivated towards achievement in his studies and recognizes that his world is a grim place. He is conditioned to compete. And he has to compete for entrance to college and continuation in it with students of a type that forty years ago would not have thought a college experience available to them. One of the effects of the G. I. Bill was to show young people that college was possible for anyone with the requisite ability, and the strong trend towards the democratization of the colleges has now reached the point where many states, and soon perhaps the federal government, will regard free higher education as the right of every young person, and consequently think it the duty of government to provide it. Certainly, the modern undergraduate is no longer the well-groomed young American who elicited the scorn of Hutchins thirty years ago. Today, students of every race and color, and of every social and economic class, swarm over the campus. It is true that the modern student is less well-dressed than the collegiate dandy of the twenties and often does not know how to behave on social occasions. But, at least in the East, he is not so deeply absorbed by the side shows of college life and rushes less eagerly into athletics, fraternities, and the multitudinous activities of the collegiate tradition. He is more often in the college library. He is nearer to reality than his father, and on the whole more concerned about national and international problems. He may frequently be seen in picket lines. He is a person of ideas and causes, occasionally a beatnik, but more often a serious and tough-minded young man. He feels, perhaps too strongly, the pressures of his time and nation and so is often betrayed into choosing those studies that would be of immediate advantage, rather than those that would serve him better in later years. But he is too shrewd to be taken in by thin disciplines in the curriculum; nor is he fooled for long by charlatans among his teachers. He is often more idealistic than the college world he enters, but is soon suggested into the practices and customs of the harsh competitive spirit he finds there, though he may secretly retain his private affections and admirations. It is a fair prediction that he will do well in the world, though he may be somewhat insensitive and at times ruthless in attaining his ends.

A word should be said about the increased aid available to students for financing education. Many college students today are enabled to pursue their education because they have been given aid through private benefactions, state scholarships, or federal loans. With the help of industry, the independent colleges have increased enormously their funds for scholarships and loans—an increase necessary as fees and tuitions rose. The states, too, have seen the wisdom of enlarging substantially their scholarship aid to students. Perhaps the most significant change in attitude has been that of the federal government. The G. I. Bill was a generous and successful act of statesmanship, though on the part of the government it was essentially a payment for past services. But Title II of the National Defense Education Act of 1958 looked forward to the general improvement of individual training. The NDEA authorized the appropriation of $47.5 million for 1959, $75 million for 1960, $82.5 million for 1961, and $90 million for 1962 to provide loans on generous terms to undergraduate and graduate students.[5] Congress, always mindful of the separation of church and state, has found it easier to aid individuals than to provide direct aid to the colleges. But before it disbanded for the Christmas vacation in 1963, Congress passed a bill to help colleges in the construction of such facilities as laboratories, libraries, classrooms, and student unions. This new bill called for an appropriation of $1.2 billion and prepared the way for further aid in the future; some of this, as we have seen, was forthcoming as the NDEA was further expanded and liberalized in 1964. It supplemented the earlier governmental acts of 1949 and 1950 (Public Law 475), which inaugurated the College Housing Loan Program for the construction of dormitories and dining halls. The whole course of these actions shows the country's deep faith in education. It also shows Congress moving cautiously towards the position that all young people eligible in point of age and ability have a right to higher education and that it is the duty of the government to provide it. Legal fictions are still needed by Congress to rationalize an action that would permit direct aid to the whole college or university.

Though each college has its special collection of problems, there are some that are common to all. For different reasons in each case, every college is pinched for funds as endowments prove no longer adequate, curriculums expand, faculty salaries rise, and costs of every kind increase. The difficulty of maintaining a teaching staff of quality is a common one, as we have seen. The problem of maintaining a liberal spirit in college studies is more pressing in the university college than in the independent college at present, but the difference cannot be counted on to last. At the moment the independent college of liberal arts is perhaps in better general health than the university college, probably because of the prosperity of the country, ample lists of qualified candidates for admission, the benefactions of private donors, the loyalty of its graduates, the energy and quality of its officers, and the indestructible spirit of dedication in its faculty. But this is the college at its best, a condition which is not universal, and the full impact of coming events has yet to be felt in most colleges.

The American graduate school is almost as confused as the college concerning its purposes, functions, and procedures, though its existence is not threatened. The major dilemma it faces is one of priorities; whether—to oversimplify, perhaps—the graduate school's primary function is education in advanced studies or the advancement of knowledge. From its Germanic origin the American graduate school received a strong tendency to regard its first duty as the extension of knowledge through research, though the conception, even in Germany, was never entirely pure. But on our shores the ideal of the advancement of knowledge for its own sake met the older ideal of service to the state and nation. The earliest and most pressing need for service was in the training of teachers for the educational establishment, a task in which the University of Michigan excelled. The conception of service to the state reached its apex in the "Wisconsin idea." Since the end of the Second World War, however, the demand by the federal government has enlarged and deepened the conception of service so vastly that the universities are in danger of losing control of their own purposes and destiny. The form of the present service for the government is, indeed, research and the advancement of knowledge, but relatively little of it is free and basic, and it does not satisfy the ideal the university holds.

In the meanwhile, though undergraduate enrollments have increased, the graduate schools have slighted the education of teachers for the colleges. The enrollments in the graduate schools have also increased proportionately, but a smaller share of the new doctors of philosophy have been attracted to college teaching. The reason for this is partly that the salaries and often the opportunities for research are greater in government and industry, especially in the sciences, engineering, and some of the social sciences. The number of doctors of philosophy teaching in the colleges has declined to approximately 24 percent of the faculty; and as a consequence the independent college has had to be content with greater proportions of men and women holding only the master's degree. The master's degree itself has increasingly become the appropriate degree for ambitious secondary-school teachers. In the colleges in universities, as we have seen, the burden of teaching has in large part fallen upon graduate assistants—a condition that is good neither for the undergraduate nor for the hard-pressed graduate student whose attention is distracted from his own educational progress.

A subtler ill of the graduate school is of long standing. Graduate schools arose at a time in history when the German universities were engaged in a strong renaissance of learning. Part of the task of modernizing knowledge before it could be successfully advanced was the assiduous collection of fact; each new fact was therefore regarded as a significant conquest. The early success of the method in virgin areas of knowledge caused the ideal of amassing facts to spread to all fields and to become a fixed technique of scholarship. The rewards at first were abundant, especially in the new fields of science, but grew scarcer and poorer in the older fields of learning as they were more intensively cultivated. The technique lingered, however, and the scholars became narrower and narrower specialists. In the study of literature, for example, this method tended to produce a barren philology, and the distinction between information and wisdom was often lost. The fact-gathering technique unfortunately has become the fixed procedure in the preparation of too many doctoral dissertations.

It is somewhat ironic that this method, which has desiccated the study of many of the humanities and social sciences, has become extremely important in the vast new areas of our ignorance that modern science has opened for research. Lately there has been some recognition of the damage that may be done by an inappropriate technique adopted from another field of study, and attempts have been made to free such studies as literature, history, and philosophy from the tyranny of an alien method. These subjects have been declining in popularity, however, and the immense premium now put upon scientific research will make their recovery difficult. The difficulty is compounded by the fact that the universities most deeply involved in research for the government are the same institutions that have in the past trained the great majority of our doctors of philosophy. In many areas of such institutions, the faculty thinks that its primary duty is to do research and begrudges the time spent upon the education of students. As a consequence, teachers for the colleges of the country are too often only casually trained.

At any rate, there has been growing recognition that the training for the doctor's degree as it is now done in our universities no longer makes it a teaching degree, but essentially a training in the techniques of research. In recent years a good deal of concern has been expressed about the appropriateness of such training for the large proportion of college teachers who do no further research once their dissertations are accepted;[6] but attempts to establish more directly appropriate training have made little progress. Possibly the independent colleges have been afraid of the damage to scholarship resulting from a training and a degree that might be regarded as second-class; and perhaps they are fearful of losing caste if they depart from an orthodox position. The graduate schools, in the firm control of established departments and professors, have shown little interest in establishing a new degree which might call for drastic revisions of course work and procedures. The most substantial changes that have occurred in the doctoral program have been two: first, the modification of the dissertation so that it may be shorter and not necessarily an original contribution to knowledge in fields where such a demand is inappropriate, but rather an exercise demonstrating the intellectual competence and skill of the candidate; and second, the inevitable broadening of the candidate's training as he undertakes new interdepartmental studies, such as comparative literature, area and language programs, combinations like American studies, or new fields in the sciences like molecular biology or geophysics.

By all odds the most significant fact concerning higher education internally has been the impact of the new scientific revolution. Externally, the most significant event has been the deep involvement of the country's strongest universities in research and training for the federal government. The number of institutions so involved is not great; one hundred of the country's two thousand colleges and universities receive 93 percent of the federal money granted for research, for graduate fellowships, and for facilities and equipment.[7] But the institutions involved are the leaders among the universities of the country, so that the impact upon higher education is strong and the effect pervasive. In the Second World War and since, the special strengths and qualities of the Massachusetts Institute of Technology made that institution one of very special value to the government.[8] The present involvement of MIT in research for the government is a highly exaggerated example and so not typical; but it does illustrate a major drift of the universities at the present time.

Founded in 1861 as an engineering and technological college, the institution profited by the Land Grant acts of 1862 and 1890. For many years MIT was well known for its eminence as an engineering school, but in the 1940s the school began to expand its interests, primarily into the area of the pure sciences but also to a limited degree into the social sciences and the humanities. For the most part, the new fields of interest were related to science and engineering in their susceptibility to measurement—economics, industrial management, communication systems, and architecture. Later the new sciences, such as biochemistry and molecular biology, have received much attention, and so has work with computers and accelerators. Formerly 80 percent of the students at MIT were enrolled in engineering programs; this figure has dropped to 40 percent as the students have gone into the pure sciences. During the Second World War, MIT became one of the nation's most important research centers, developing radar, air defenses, and missiles, and was deeply involved in nuclear physics. So successful was the relationship in research between MIT and the government that, since the war, the operation has been perpetuated and expanded. Today the institution manages and staffs the following scientific laboratories for the government: the Laboratory of Insulation Research, the Research Laboratory of Electronics, the Lincoln Laboratory, and (with Harvard) the Cambridge Electron Accelerator.[9] In 1959–60 MIT received a total of $65.8 million from the government for all purposes. One may detect a nostalgic pining for a simpler day in the comment that MIT has made upon the situation: "Only our overriding sense of national duty can justify our assumption of obligations of such an order."[10] Yet this figure was less than the total granted to another institution, $122 million to the University of California at Berkeley, plus $695 million granted for the construction and operation of the Los Alamos Laboratory.

The ineluctable fact is that, for better or for worse, the Massachusetts Institute of Technology has been changed in its essential nature. Formerly mainly an undergraduate college, it is now more notable for its graduate school. Indeed, it is now more a research center than an educational institution. The achievements of MIT have been recognized by the government, industry, and the public; it is the favorite of the scientific world, and riches have been heaped upon it. Its recent drive for funds netted $98 million, a sum greater than that raised by any other American educational institution and $32 million more than the goal set. To these palpable assets must be added the intense intellectual activity of the place, which is single-minded in its dedication to the increase of scientific knowledge. It is a center for powerful scientific minds, both among its faculty and its students. The debits of the MIT situation are the darker side of its virtues. The members of the faculty, typifying the new breed of scientists, are so intent upon their specialties that they have little time to contemplate more general issues or to relate their scientific concerns with those of humanity at large. The busy faculty member is often not available to the student. The preoccupation with intellectual activity to the exclusion of other aspects of life infects the campus, and the buildings have been called dingy and grim, with little beauty in the miles of corridors, and the students supercilious in their supposed superiority to undergraduates elsewhere. The MIT administration has long been aware of the narrowness in the educational experience offered to the undergraduates and has valiantly striven to impose one course in either the humanities or the social sciences upon the student each semester. Inevitably, such courses seem to the serious student to be interruptions. Inevitably, too, the faculty that teaches these secondary courses does not equal the scientific faculty in eminence, though MIT has been able to attract a number of distinguished scholars in such subjects as economics and political science.

As I have said, the relations of MIT with the government present us with an exaggerated case—a condition that judicious men at MIT do not contemplate with unalloyed happiness. The inspection of such a case, however, does allow us to see what has happened to some extent in the twenty-five universities that are most deeply involved in serving the federal government by sponsored research and development, and to a lesser degree in the additional seventy-five institutions that share with them the government grants and contracts. The size of the government's operations in the colleges and universities, and the limiting effect of contracts and project research on basic research, have alarmed the scientists themselves, and there has recently been a good deal of outspoken criticism. This most recent unhappiness is quite different from the older complaints, which mainly consisted of dissatisfaction with the government's arrangements for such matters as overhead, administrative red-tape, problems of tenure, and imbalance in the faculties. The new criticisms come from the scientists themselves and are directed at the dilution of scientific training caused by the sheer numbers of scientists and engineers demanded, and by the neglect of teaching in the sciences because of the preoccupation of the faculties with government research.[11] It seems at times as if science is as careless of its future as it has been of its past.

It would assuredly be unfair, however, not to acknowledge the benefits that have come to the universities from project research. Most universities feel that by reason of government support their research capacities have been enlarged and improved, their faculties in the sciences have benefited, especially in salaries and working conditions, and the work of graduate students and postdoctoral fellows has been generously financed.[12] Of special pleasure to the scientists is the fact that summer salaries have been made possible. It must be acknowledged, too, that the government demand for scientists and other scholars has had the effect of raising salaries for the whole academic profession; and one can detect very little resentment of the present situation on the part of nonscientists. Most faculty people realize that, if government funds for research were withdrawn, the staff would shrink and research vital to the country would have to be abandoned. It is hoped, however, that Congress will see the need for supporting basic research; for in this area we have drawn dangerously upon our capital of ideas.

A few observations need to be made upon the many professional schools and special institutes. The greater part of them in this country have tended to cluster about universities, and increasingly so as the years move towards the twenty-first century. The most obvious fact about such schools and organizations, however, is their rapid proliferation. Almost every occupation that has any pretension to a special body of learning, or even a special technique, has found somewhere a university that is willing to sponsor it. To the older divisions of the university that rested upon the arts and sciences—divinity, medicine, law, and later engineering and agriculture—there have been added schools of architecture, music, drama, library, nursing, teaching, journalism, business, and hotel management, to name only a few of those accepted by our strongest universities. One shrinks from naming schools for undertakers, hairdressers, dietitians, and athletic coaches, which, nevertheless, do exist. In the debasement of higher education, the central university itself is not free from blame. One need only read the lists of titles that have been approved as acceptable theses for the doctor's degree to realize the deterioration of the ideal of learning.

To these many schools associated with institutions of higher learning, one must add the considerable number of praiseworthy independent institutes devoted to research, usually in some special field like biological science and health, international relations, economics, the classics, or behavioral sciences. One thinks immediately of such distinguished institutes as the Rockefeller, Carnegie, and Brookings. Such institutes are often first-rate in the quality of their research and in their influence on learning, though it is not always in their design to further the process of education. Many of them, however, are of great aid to the universities and colleges in maintaining high standards in the fields of their interest.

If the proliferation of professional schools is an obvious fact in American education, the most admirable feature is the steady improvement in the quality of standards and achievement of the older professional schools of divinity, medicine, law, and engineering. As we have seen, these schools are increasingly able to demand a longer and better undergraduate training from their applicants for admission, as well as a higher quality of talent and motivation. A word about each of these major kinds of professional schools may be useful.

Probably the study of law is now attracting more young men of ability than any other profession. This is natural enough, for success in the law often leads directly to wealth and frequently to power in the national government. The number of legally trained men in

Congress and the great offices of state far surpasses that of any other profession. Then, too, the study of law, which was as dusty and routine as any study could be fifty years ago, has been completely renovated. The older conception that the law was an almost change-less set of rules for the student to learn by rote has been replaced by the idea that the law is a natural growth of human society and changes to answer the varying conditions and tempers of the culture that sustains it. The best law schools in recent years have tended to become schools for the advanced study of the social sciences, and in the faculties of such schools one finds economists, political scientists, sociologists, psychologists, and philosophers. It is natural, therefore, that the greatest law schools are in our greatest universities; and it would be extremely difficult for a law school to be great without the rich intellectual life of a university to support it. The curriculum of the modern law school, with its breadth and relevance, has proved to be an admirable training not only for legal practice, but also for leadership in government and industry and in the management of the affairs of our universities and colleges.

The great leap forward that the medical schools of America achieved as a result of Abraham Flexner's magnificent prescription for them[13] has made this country foremost in the world in medical science. This is attested by the numbers of medical men and students from all over the world who come to study American techniques and procedures. The quality, scope, and interest of our medical education has been much improved by the immense amount of money that has been poured into medical research by agencies of the federal government, philanthropic foundations, and the public. The tremendous increase in knowledge and the improvement of techniques in the field support the hope, which has almost become an expectancy, that some great discovery that will eliminate human suffering is about to be made. The study of medicine is made more attractive to young people, too, by the fact that they enter almost immediately as students into the practice of their profession as junior partners of their teachers. It is little wonder that, in spite of the heavy costs of training and the long years of apprenticeship required of them, candidates for admission have besieged the medical schools in great numbers.

But recently a change has been noticeable. The number and quality of the candidates for admission has declined, and this fact confronts the poorer medical schools with disaster and causes alarm in some of the more substantial ones. The reason for the decline is probably that the area of the pure sciences—physics in particular—has since World War II become much more attractive as a career to scientifically minded students. In any case, the decline has caused concern in the nation because the medical schools are not producing physicians, especially internists, in nearly sufficient numbers for the health of the country. The able young medical man is inevitably attracted by the magnificent opportunities for research, supported lavishly by the National Institutes of Health, or by the glittering prospect of becoming a specialist in a lucrative field. The major fact about our medical schools, however, is that they have become immense, complex, and extremely expensive centers of research in an area of knowledge that is of the deepest concern to humanity.

The times are not equally propitious for the third traditional professional study, theology. The divinity schools of the nation, fewer and less appreciated than the law or medical schools, have had to scramble for students, and indeed have drawn on general university resources in order to award scholarships to almost all their candidates for admission. Furthermore, these schools have not been able to attract the ablest students from the colleges in appreciable numbers. Their curriculums have been expanded, often into programs of social service, Sunday-school teaching, and other less than rigorous studies, at the expense of more exacting learning. Nonetheless, in those cases where the theological schools have escaped immediate domination by a religious sect, and especially in those that are a part of a university, the richness, rationality, and modernity of the training has greatly improved. As in the case of the law and medical schools con-

nected with universities, the association with other fields of learning
—history, literature, philosophy, psychology—has been beneficial to
divinity schools and has provided balance, perspective, tolerance,
and rationality to an area of study that is all too vulnerable to preju-
dices, passions, and stubborn ignorance. It is hardly necessary to add
that divinity schools which honor and practice rigorous scholarship
and make religious instruction viable in the present age are greatly
to be cherished.

The Morrill Act of 1862, establishing the Land Grant colleges for
the improvement of the agricultural and mechanical arts, added new
dimensions to education in America. Before 1862 most of the engineering projects that were undertaken were by military engineers
trained at West Point. It may generally be said that the engineering
and agricultural schools created by the Morrill Act prospered best
when they were a part of a comprehensive university, as one may
readily see in such examples as Cornell University and the University
of Wisconsin. But there was one grave flaw in the situation. In 1862
few institutions, even those calling themselves universities, were able
to give advanced work in engineering and agriculture, even if students sufficiently trained could have been found to take such work.
They were established, accordingly, as undergraduate schools and
programs, and only in our own time has the training in engineering
and applied science begun to take on in full form the advanced work
appropriate to a profession. In the best engineering schools the
tendency is to make the undergraduate phase of engineering a major,
firmly based on mathematics and the physical sciences, and then to
encourage the prospective engineer towards further study. The fact
that the Soviet Union is producing more technically trained students
called engineers need not worry us unduly if our own engineers are
more highly trained, though it is likely that we shall have to create
more vocational schools to produce the needed technicians. In a
lesser degree, the same problems faced the agricultural divisions
of the Land Grant schools, but the rapid advances of biology and

chemistry have lifted this branch of learning to the professional level of the sciences. The results may be seen in the magnificent teaching and research in agriculture in a number of our great state universities.

A briefer comment must now be made upon a few of the other schools that train significant numbers of students for the professions. First, the schools of education, which have been subjected to much criticism in recent years. They are, of course, among the newer professional schools and are more peculiarly American institutions than most of the others. The chief function of these schools has been to produce teachers for secondary and primary schools. The colleges of liberal arts and sciences have seldom gone to schools of education to recruit faculty members. The schools of education were founded on an immature psychology and allowed themselves to become uncritical advocates of a permissiveness that was characterized by opponents as looseness and by themselves as progressive. Their patron saint was John Dewey, whose pragmatic doctrine they did not fully comprehend. They have been criticized as democratic to the point of being indiscriminately egalitarian and as lacking any rigorous standards. In sober fact, whether as cause or consequence, these schools have had to draw large numbers of their students from a less gifted and less privileged sector of our society; and the rewards and honors of the teaching profession have not been attractive. In recent years many of these schools, especially those not attached to universities, have abandoned the title of teachers' colleges and, without much internal change, have advertised themselves as colleges of liberal arts and sciences. The teaching in our secondary schools is probably the weakest link in the country's educational system, and, until successful teaching in the high schools is cared for and honored proportionately to its importance, the whole system of education will suffer. The colleges or universities have little right to complain of the situation, for long ago they abandoned the field and sought more glamorous but less important goals.

Other schools of a more specialized function and less national impact have flourished and have sometimes added materially to the culture and happiness of the country. One thinks immediately of the schools and conservatories of music, the schools and departments of drama and painting, and, of a more utilitarian purpose, the schools for training in architecture, forestry, and librarianship. It is not likely, I think, that the geniuses in music, art, and the theater of the future will often be found in these schools, but the general level of American culture will be raised and a climate may be created in which these arts will flourish. The immediate achievements of our schools of forestry in such vital areas as conservation and the improvement of watersheds and quality of building materials need no defense. The demands of the training for architecture, as for forestry, are so numerous and so diverse that the multitudinous resources of a university seem necessary for the adequate training of students in this important field.

There is a difference, however, between a profession and a technique. A profession requires the mastery of a formidable body of learning; a technique is a slighter skill, asking for less demanding qualities and knowledge, however useful the field may be. Library schools, for example, play their most valuable part in assisting other branches of scholarship. One may be more reluctant to justify schools of journalism and mass communication and may think that a sound education in writing and speaking in the school and college years, and a knowledge in some depth in a substantial field of human activity, would be a better training for these skills. This list of special schools could be extended indefinitely, and those mentioned above are only the most prominent.

Among the innumerable new schools and departments of study, there is one that is uniquely American and characteristic of our time and culture. This is the higher study of business and industry for the purpose of achieving better management and better understanding of the relation between the several parts of industry, such as management and labor, production and wages, capitalization and profit. The primary base of such studies is, of course, practical economics, but often psychology is added, as well as engineering, statistics, and computer analysis. The laboratory for such studies is the present industrial and commercial activity of the country, or indeed of the world. These studies are likely to be intensely practical and to take little cognizance of history beyond the recent two or three decades. At the undergraduate level, the programs are usually designated by some such title as industrial administration, but at the advanced stage the title and range of subjects are enlarged as the studies move towards a professional status. The field is popular with young Americans because it is in close accord with the values of American life, and with its needs. Our industrial and commercial society has become so complex that there is an ever increasing need for men and women of perception, profundity, and character to guide its operation. For business to become a true profession, however, a larger and more systematic philosophy must inform the schools of business, and more effective and rigorous methods of research must be developed and practiced.

As one looks, as from a hill, over the wide field of higher education in America at the present time, one must inevitably be impressed by the energy, the vitality, and the ceaseless motion that goes on before one's eyes. One must also recognize the immediate usefulness of most of this activity. These qualities are representative of the American temper and character, and our higher education faithfully reflects our society. What one misses is any sense of design in the multitudinous motion, or any discriminating appreciation of quality. Nationally, our institutions range from the height of excellence to an abysmal vulgarity, and the public does not seem to know the difference. The noble conception of democracy and equal opportunity and justice for all seems to have degenerated into an undiscriminating judgment of values and abilities. It is a common notion, endlessly expressed, that education is the cure for all our ills. It will do much, to be sure, but to do well what it can do it must be a wise and balanced education, in which all the parts are taught in a liberal spirit with a constant awareness of history and philosophy to give direction to our thinking. During the last several centuries we have been living in an age of science and profiting enormously therefrom in national security, health, and material well-being. We have no intention of losing those benefits or of losing an appreciation for the rationality and the clarity of spirit that science has given us. All our feelings, thoughts, and actions are profoundly affected by the pervasive scientific spirit and the scientific way of looking at life. At the present time the scientific culture itself tends to be somewhat aggressive and arrogant. The faults of the older literary, historical, and philosophical culture were pride, complacency, and an ill-founded sense of superiority— qualities that led to snobbery and stagnation. But there were virtues in the old culture that could be useful to the new—such qualities as perspective, form and beauty, a sense of proportion and purpose, a deep knowledge of man, going beyond his physical attributes to his heart and spirit. Nor did the older culture lack an exacting scholarship of its own. One would plead now that our education, from the primary grades through the doctorate, would join the good aspects of the new and old cultures in a fresh and liberal design, with each recognizing in generous proportions the necessity for the other. Neither by itself is sufficiently ample for the good life. This is a hope, rather than a possibility that will be soon achieved.

Many questions about higher education have to be left with tentative answers at best, for we are viewing something that is intensely alive and moving very fast. The continuing problem of higher education in America will be to achieve and retain a balance between breadth and specialization. In our present condition, specialization is dominant and will go forward on its own momentum. It is for the breadth traditionally provided by the college of liberal arts that care needs to be taken. In recent years the liberal-arts college has once more been severely challenged. Its passing would be more than the end of an epoch; it would be the loss of a way of life that would leave the country poorer in spirit. As John Stuart Mill observed long ago, a man needs to be a wise man before he can be a good lawyer, physician, or indeed a good specialist of any kind. Very recently the challenge has diminished, for many of our greatest scientists and scholars are now speaking out for the necessity for breadth in education; but the way to restore it is still to be found. Today, the primary need of our educational institutions, from the smallest private college of liberal arts to the huge public multiversity, is for academic leaders of high intelligence and magnanimous spirit who will work to achieve this wholesome balance.

EPILOGUE | THE DILEMMA
OF NATIONAL GREATNESS

As the dust settles, the most significant fact about Sir Charles Snow's *The Two Cultures* is the passionate interest it aroused in both England and America.[1] It is less astonishing that in reaction there rose a kind of conspiracy to deny that a rift in our culture exists at all. This means, I think, that Snow said something perhaps not altogether satisfactorily, but something nevertheless very near the surface of consciousness of the two societies. This was especially true of England, for the intellectual British have been searching since the First World War, and more intensively since the Second, for the underlying causes of their disastrously inadequate performance in both those wars, and the disintegration of their sunlit empire. To England her loss of greatness and power was a grim reality; to America it was a lesson to be drawn from the unfortunate history of a kinsman and friend.

The idea that there are two competing aspects of our culture is not a new one. It is at least as old as Francis Bacon's *New Atlantis,* when the older literary culture, derived from Greece and Italy, was challenged by the new science. The literary humanistic aspect of the culture of the West, however, had entrenched itself in academies, schools, and universities, the Typhoid Marys of culture, and these until the nineteenth century allowed little room in their curriculums for science. Scientific achievement was an individual matter, and often a lonely effort. But the march of the scientific mind was the prime achievement of the nineteenth century, and from time to time the dominant humanistic aspect of the culture was severely challenged. More than any other work, Darwin's *The Origin of Species* shook traditional thinking and provided the immediate base for a new challenge—a conflict in which both sides behaved in a manner that has become characteristic. Thomas Henry Huxley belligerently announced that science was by far the most important part of our culture and demanded an almost exclusive priority for it in the educational process. He denied the usefulness of literature, history, and philosophy. An even less temperate scientist than Huxley, John Tyndall, in his famous "Belfast Address" in 1874 pushed the attack into the sacred area of theology. "By an intellectual necessity," he said, "I cross the boundary of the experimental evidence, and discern in that matter which we, in our ignorance of its latent powers, and notwithstanding our professed reverence for its Creator, have hitherto covered with opprobrium, the promise and potency of all terrestial life. . . . We claim, and we shall wrest, from theology, the entire domain of cosmological theory. All schemes and systems which thus infringe upon the domain of science, must, *in so far as they do this,* submit to its control, and relinquish all thought of controlling it."[2] Though it may seem now that Tyndall need not have been so aggressive about it, he was no doubt right. So, too, was Huxley in his contention that our study of the real world should be accorded a much larger place in education, for science not only supplied the useful knowledge needed by an industrial and practical age, but indeed went even further and supplied the basis for its philosophical thinking and its ethical assumptions.

The champions of science of the nineteenth century, however, had not fully estimated the forensic skill and the cool capacity of the champion of the humanistic aspect of culture. Matthew Arnold was a veteran in this kind of fencing. In his "Literature and Science" he followed the classic principles of debate.[3] He conceded that the ascendancy of the nonscientific disciplines perpetuated an aristocratic point of view which could no longer be fully effective in a modern society. But as he moved to the offensive he asserted that neither he nor any other sensible person had ever contended that culture meant merely the elegant study of belles-lettres. The culture of a nation, he said, includes its whole intellectual activity. He did not believe that science could ever usurp the place of the humanistic studies because such a change would neglect the powers that make for quality in human life—its conduct, its intellect and imagination, its beauty, its social life and manners. True knowledge of how to live does not depend upon scientific knowledge of the universe, but rather upon those studies which man has pursued for two thousand years, even in ages when his scientific ideas were most fantastic. A modern culture must include science; the danger was that the aggressiveness of the new science would leave no room for the humanistic and social studies. By his intolerably sweet reasonableness—and with the help of public inertia—Arnold prevailed and thereby further delayed an adjustment that should have taken place in English education a hundred years ago.

By his victory, of course, Arnold had only scotched the challenge, not killed it. In the next phase speculation entered the popular imagination. H. G. Wells, sometimes a prophet and sometimes a historian, was always a teller of tales. In his fine and imaginative story, "The Time Machine," he is deeply concerned with the two competing aspects of the culture, the humanistic and the applied scientific. In effect, Wells projects into the far future the two aspects of the culture as he sees them in England at the turn of the century. The traveler in time comes through thousands of years to find that the population of England is made up of two different races of human beings. On the surface of the earth, living among the ruins of ancient splendor, are the Eloi, diminutive, infantile, beautiful creatures who spend their days dancing in the sun. They are incapable of sustained attention; a minute or two, and their minds have wandered away to some other trivial matter. They neither toil nor spin, but live upon the fruits of the abundant trees. Their nights, however, are spent in a very different fashion. Fearful of the dark, they huddle together as they sleep in the ruins of their once great civilization. There are the indulgent humanists of Wells's day, extrapolated into their distant future.

But more fearsome than the dark are the Morlocks, the other inhabitants of that far-off future—the grimy creatures who inhabit the bowels of the earth and who come up from their gloomy regions to prey upon the shuddering and helpless Eloi as they sleep. For the childish and ephemeral Eloi, like the children of Ireland, are worth herding as a supply of food for their masters. The dark dwellers of Wells's underworld are not scientists; they have been projected into the future only as applied scientists. Their dusky world hums with machinery for ventilation, such light as they need and can endure, and other continuing necessities of life. The inhabitants of this lower world are grim creatures who have lost all the better attributes of humanity and have developed only their appetite and cruelty. They were once possessors of a science, for their technology is built upon it, but there is no sign now of the curiosity and imagination that inform science. As the Eloi have progressed in their deterioration by an ever increasing indulgence of their softer natures, so these denizens of the underground have progressed in their mechanistic qualities, gradually losing their humanity.

Wells was not primarily interested in making a prophecy, I think, nor was he especially interested in a subtle analysis of the tendencies he could clearly see in the British nation at the beginning of the present century. Here, as elsewhere, he was chiefly concerned to tell a story that would engage the imagination of the reading public. Still, he saw these trends—on the one hand, the relatively small group of the aristocracy and gentry leading recklessly indulgent lives, dancing in the sun of their wealth and peace, and parasitically careless of the industrial and technological sources of their imperial power; and on the other side, the crude, aggressive, and narrowly educated class from which British society now drew such technologists as it possessed. Wells was not a member by birth or wealth of the social and political establishment that controlled all the major institutions of the nation—Parliament, industry, the army and navy, and education—and that strove to exclude all who had not attended the great public schools. It is not clear that Wells saw the extent of the dry rot that had eaten into British society in the years before 1914. As we may see in Wells's longer novels, his sympathies were with the small business and the working classes. And yet by profession Wells was deeply engaged in the literary aspect of culture, and he undoubtedly saw and disliked the inevitable assumption of power by the crude and insensitive technologists.

We can see now by the clearer vision which hindsight allows that England, who had been the great pioneer of the Industrial Revolution and upon that strong base had won and confirmed her empire, had rested upon her laurels and had ceased to go forward in technology and industry in the last quarter of the nineteenth century. While England slept, first Germany and then America took over the leadership in technology, industry, and commerce. British society had favored the gentleman over the industrialist, making a sharp distinction between the two. In the navy and army, appointment and advancement were gained by connections and wealth. Altogether, a man's birth and class were more important than the service he performed for society. These values were clearly reflected in education, which is the arrangement society makes for the perpetuation of its culture; and here at the highest level the arts were cultivated to the neglect of the sciences. And since the future of a country, as we have now come to see so clearly, rests upon the intelligence and training of its people, this was a very serious matter. An extremely small proportion of the people were educated in the older aspects of the culture at Oxford and Cambridge and a few other universities, and the great mass of the people were given a cheap training that taught little technology or business. Even the universities and the public schools that fed them gave short shrift to science and applied science, if indeed the subjects were taught at all. The graduates were trained to become diplomats and colonial rulers and politicians. These were of course worthy tasks in themselves, but the neglect of science and technology meant that little talent was trained to serve adequately the industrial sources of national strength, and little research was undertaken to improve the techniques and materials of peace or war.

Even after Prussia had shown her might in 1871, a technological stagnation similar to England's continued in France. But Germany, united as a nation and intellectually ablaze with the new learning, science, and technology, began preparing for the fierce struggle for power which she saw as inevitable as the twentieth century approached. For the conditions of national greatness in the modern industrial world are inescapable: science, technology, endless research and hard work, ambition and aggressiveness, and the search for talent wherever it may be found. These are the ingredients for great power. They do not make for comfort and the quiet life; nor do most of them make for good manners and peace.

In his distinguished book, *The Swordbearers: Studies in Supreme Command in the First World War*,[4] Correlli Barnett allots a quarter of the volume to an account of Sir John Jellicoe, the British commander at the Battle of Jutland. The subtitle of the appraisal of Jellicoe is significant: "Sailor with a Flawed Cutlass." The whole book is one that should be read by all concerned with national power —by statesmen and politicians who shape the policies that may lead to war, industrialists who fashion the implements of war, and the military forces that have to conduct it. Quite as important, the book should be studied by the leaders of education who prepare all these men for the crisis. When Jellicoe was placed in command of the British Grand Fleet, a few days before the war began, he knew that his forces were numerically superior to the German High Seas Fleet. He also knew what few in the Admiralty, the government, or the navy knew—that in many respects the English fleet was inferior, in the design of its ships, in submarines, in torpedoes, mines, guns, and shells. Worse still, the British navy was inferior in the talent and training of its officers, for the navy, the pride and protection of the nation, was the preserve of the well-born and the wealthy. Appointment and advancement depended upon class, nepotism, and favoritism. The navy that had the reputation of being the greatest in the world had become little more than "an exclusive yacht club." Many of the officers were men, like Beatty who ultimately succeeded Jellicoe, of dash and spirit, still thinking of battle in the terms of Nelson. Like Churchill himself at the Admiralty, they were frequently brilliant as improvisers, strong in spirit, but often disastrously lacking in experience and in a comprehension of strategy. In the opinion of Barnett, the Battle of Jutland was a defeat for British technology, but he goes further in his comment: "More than that, as with the French at Crécy and Sedan, a social system had been exposed by battle as decadent and uncreative. Jutland proves that already in 1914, when Britain and her empire had never seemed richer, more powerful, more technologically able, dry rot was crumbling the inner structure of the vast mansion."[5]

The ultimate accounting was delayed by the victory of the Allies in 1918, in large part owing to Jellicoe himself and the Grand Fleet. To Barnett the spectacular collapse of British industry, power, and empire after the Second World War was not a sudden disaster but had been long preparing. The Battle of Jutland was merely "the final acute phase of seventy years of decline. For the principal armed service of a country—in its professional attitudes, its equipment, its officer corps—is an extension, a reflection, of that country's whole society, and especially of its dominating groups."[6] One may add to Barnett's indictment that the British army in the First World War was in no better case than the navy, and extend the time of the onset of decay to the Crimean War and the charge of the Light Brigade at Balaklava.

But inventive, clever, and thorough as the Germans were in their technology, organization, and training, they made a fundamental mistake in high policy that defeated all their military preparations.

Wisdom was not with them when they conceived and built their High Seas Fleet, for they built a fleet just large enough to be provocative and alarming to the British, but not strong enough to defeat the Grand Fleet. The result was that as soon as the war began Germany's commercial fleet was driven from the seas, her colonies and markets lost, and ultimately a severe shortage of food and other crucial supplies was created at home. The education of the leaders of Germany, unquestionably the first nation in the world in the late nineteenth century in scientific and technological achievement, was lacking in breadth and was specialized to a degree that, however efficient they were in the immediate circumstances, inhibited a larger view. The makers of German high policy in the First World War, as again in the Second, seemed to lack the wisdom, perspective, and above all the understanding of human nature which (far beyond psychology) a study of biography, history, and literature would have given them. If one may presume to prescribe for the German mind, one would insist upon a deep study of hubris, that quality best seen in the works of the great tragic dramatists, ancient and modern. A lack of understanding can be as fatal as a lack of knowledge.

To one like myself, inclined to read the character, quality, vigor, and intelligence of a nation most clearly in the education it provides for its people, such history is most illuminating. For a hundred years after 1810, when the University of Berlin was founded, German universities made their country the intellectual capital of the world, the place to which scholars and scientists looked first for light and leading. Here was to be found the new learning and the new method, deeply grounded upon science and intensely professional. By contrast, English education was stagnant and uncreative. Of course, England had its scientific geniuses—Lyell, Darwin, Faraday, Maxwell, Kelvin, Rutherford—but many of these men were not actively connected with universities and their work was done elsewhere. Oxford and Cambridge, which set the tone for education, were deeply immersed in the college system and had not found the way to become true modern universities. Moreover, until very late they offered to an almost exclusive degree only the literary, humanistic aspects of education—the older culture that Huxley had wished to see displaced. It is true, of course, that this traditional education was one of very considerable quality in itself, producing a fine race of statesmen, diplomats, managers of colonies, scholars, thinkers, artists, and writers. True, the greatness of nations and civilizations as history recognizes it is to be found in the accomplishments of just such men. They may sometimes provide wisdom in the conduct of war and policy, but not often now are they the sinews of power. It may be possible to be a small, weak, and happy nation, eminent in the arts that make life interesting and gracious, but such a nation can at the same time hardly aspire to be a first-rate power in our competitive world.

This is England's dilemma. In the hope that England can recover her greatness among modern nations, C. P. Snow advocates a new culture and education, built upon science and technology, which will replace the customary programs of British education. Like Tyndall and Huxley before him, he wants a great deal. Perhaps such a demand is inevitable in circumstances where tradition is so entrenched and where the new has been so long frustrated from gaining even a respectable place in the curriculum. It has taken two devastating wars and the loss of an empire to shake the tradition; but now a new challenge is given, and this time it may have more effect than it has had before.

The pertinence to America and American education of either the Battle of Jutland or the advantages and deficits of English and German education in the last one hundred and fifty years may not be immediately apparent, but I believe it is real. The colonial colleges of New England and Virginia were founded upon the English models, and the influence of Oxford and Cambridge went a good deal deeper than external organization. That influence determined the direction of the studies, and the curriculum of the American colleges for more than two centuries was heavily traditional and literary. This education aimed to prepare preachers, lawyers, and statesmen to serve and guide the nation. The ideal and the means of achieving it are still strong in our Eastern educational institutions. By and large, the students in the colleges of the Ivy League and in the smaller private colleges of the region major in history, English and American literature, philosophy, political science, and economics, and the larger part of the talent of these colleges is headed for law and industry. These students look forward to being the managers of our society in government, business, and industry, as their fathers have been before them and are now. Yet the dangers we have seen in British education have not been altogether absent in these American institutions. They, too, have until relatively recently been the preserve of the wealthy—exclusive clubs where place was obtained by inheritance. Only lately has an aroused awareness of the true necessities of the nation made the colleges less receptive to preferential demands, and many a bewildered parent today has a feeling of being betrayed by the old school when there is no place there for his son. Only lately, too, has keen competition spurred the younger graduates of these colleges to see that a more rigorous and extended training and a higher level of performance is required of them if they are to hold their place in an aggressive society.

In the nineteenth century, however, a movement of great significance in American higher education took place—the rise of universities based upon the German model, particularly the University of Berlin; and here again the foreign influence went far beyond structure and organization. It affected the very habit of university life and largely dictated the content and methods of the studies. A scientific ideal permeated all fields, even the humanistic ones, and professors became professionals, dedicated to research. Indeed, the ideal of research and the accompanying interest in its technical applications were prevalent everywhere. In Wisconsin and Michigan, for example, the universities were dedicated to direct service to the commonwealth. Such older universities as Yale and Harvard established special schools for the study of science and technology. War, whose main effect is destruction, often creates; and the Civil War did much both in disclosing to the nation the great need for an improved technology and in getting it off to a fast start. Like the educational system of Germany, the university movement emphasized specialization and professional training, usually to the slighting of the broader liberal studies. It was characteristic of the trend that Johns Hopkins, the university leader of the country for a time, only reluctantly came to see the necessity for an undergraduate college. In Germany, the student hastened from the Gymnasium to his professional studies in the university. In the new American universities he often went directly into engineering or science from high school, or entered a combined program that provided him with a more immediate profession than did the program in liberal arts. The trend has gone so far that in many institutions the student is still inclined to think of literature, history, and philosophy as studies suitable only for girls.

Under the competitive pressures of today, both national and individual, intense specialization has increased in every college in the country, and some colleges, acting in ignorance or panic, have allowed the humanistic studies to be crowded into a minimal place in their students' programs. We need academic statesmen, men who will be able to comprehend and fuse these trends from our early and our more recent past into the one great culture of which they are really only parts. The culture of a nation creates its education; in turn, the education of a nation enters into the creation of the ever renewed culture. It is the part of wisdom to see the culture as one continuous totality, as it surely is, rather than to sharpen the issues between its different parts. The need for the scientific and technological aspect is vital if we are to survive and prosper, but the strength and virtues of the tradition that has built a deep idealism into the American character over the generations should be neither belittled nor cast out.

The two strands in the educational aspect of our culture, the humanistic derived from England and the scientific from Germany, are in uneasy balance in our colleges today. The hard struggles of war and politics abroad and the fierce competition at home since 1940 have elevated the newer aspect into a position of dominance. But the tradition and substance of learning that has served Western civilization so well for twenty-five hundred years cannot be ignored, and surely there should be ample room for both in the educational plan of a nation that aspires to greatness.

If America is to be renowned in history for the wisdom of her leadership among the nations as well as for her competence in protecting her people and the sources of her power, her men and women must be educated greatly.

C. P. Snow's challenge of the traditional culture, deeply embedded in the English educational system, rose, I think, from his distress at the startling decline of his nation's power in this century, and from his hope of providing a method of recovery through a rigorous new education and culture. Undoubtedly, an element of desperation enters into his proposed cure; and there are advantages as well as necessities in his panacea. But there would be losses of an incalculable sort, too, if England, in her eagerness to regain her power, should abandon altogether the values she has traditionally contributed to our world.

Today, the whirligig of time has elevated the United States into the position once held by Britain; and we are committed as a nation to maintain our place of power and glory in a material world. This fact, of course, has far-reaching implications. One of these is that our institutions must be more than just kept up to date, especially the education and training of our people. Another is that we must allot a huge proportion of our wealth to research, to science and technology, for the maintenance of our power abroad and our health and welfare at home. But to go headlong in the pursuit of power to the exclusion of other values has many dangers. We may easily slip into the ugly posture of Sparta or Prussia and become a curse and a by-word to the world. This would be painful to us, for we would have to give up our naive hope of being loved as a nation. Already to our bewilderment we are feared and hated in many parts of the world. Mastership is paid for at a high cost.

And we have that much older commitment to consider—the early and lasting commitment we have given to democracy. There are subtler implications here than our national resolve to provide public education for all as far as each student is capable of taking it. We must actively search out talent wherever it may be found in our population and take the greatest care to keep the way open for that talent to rise. In these operations, our schools and colleges have already acknowledged their heavy obligations. But there are dangers here, too. One is that in our yearning for equality our judgments may become sentimental. A far greater danger lies in man's very human instinct, under the pressures of a very diverse society, to favor his caste, his relatives and friends, and to form exclusive enclaves in the manner of English society. This tendency is evident in the closed organization of our political parties, local and national, in the interlocking directorates of our industrial corporations, and sometimes in the boards of our colleges and universities. If we are to keep the morale of our society healthy, that society must be free, democratic, and open. There should be little room for exclusion of any kind in our public institutions. And this, too, is part of the cost of power.

Fortunately for us, America is not now under the stern compulsion of Britain to regain power, and we do not have to think of our culture as half scientific and half humanistic, with a choice that must be made between the two parts. To drive singlemindedly for the scientific aspects of culture would probably secure our power in the world, but would cost too much in terms of human life and happiness. We are in a position where we can aspire to a single culture, comprehending the total intellectual activity of man—and his mode of living, too, in the broadened definition of culture that modern anthropology has given us. We are fortunate in our geography, in our people with their mixed and generally healthy traditions, and above all in the vast resources that permit us to develop all aspects of culture. If we can make a harmonious whole of our mixed heritage instead of deepening the rift, we might create in this green and pleasant land something much more worthy in the eye of history than a great cult of power—that is, a civilization great in the arts of peace as well as war.

> O, it is excellent
> To have a giant's strength; but it is tyrannous
> To use it like a giant.[7]

So, from the older aspect of culture in his and Bacon's time, spoke Shakespeare, lending his wisdom to the newer.

BIBLIOGRAPHY | NOTES | INDEX

BIBLIOGRAPHY

In the notes to this volume I refer to the books dealing with separate colleges and universities as they are discussed in the text, and I have therefore not thought it necessary to list them in this bibliographical section. In the last three decades a great deal of excellent historical work has been done, especially upon single institutions in the context of American history. A few that are both comprehensive and significant should be mentioned here:

Becker, Carl, *Cornell University: Founders and the Founding*. Ithaca: Cornell University Press, 1943.

Bicentennial History of Columbia University, 15 vols., by many hands. New York: Columbia University Press, 1954–1957.

Cheyney, Edward Potts, *History of the University of Pennsylvania, 1740–1940*. Philadelphia: University of Pennsylvania Press, 1940.

Curti, Merle, and Vernon Carstensen, *The University of Wisconsin: A History, 1849–1925*, 2 vols. Madison: University of Wisconsin Press, 1949.

French, John C., *A History of the University Founded by Johns Hopkins*. Baltimore: Johns Hopkins University Press, 1946.

Morison, Samuel Eliot, *Three Centuries of Harvard, 1636–1936*. Cambridge: Harvard University Press, 1936.

Pierson, George Wilson, *Yale: College and University, 1871–1937*, 2 vols. New Haven: Yale University Press, 1952–1955.

Sagendorph, Kent, *Michigan: The Story of the University*. New York: E. P. Dutton, 1948.

Wertenbaker, Thomas Jefferson, *Princeton, 1746–1896*. Princeton: Princeton University Press, 1946.

It will be observed that most of the works named above mark a stage in the institution's maturity and that the histories were prepared to mark a significant occasion. Many of the colleges in every part of the country have also added distinguished volumes to a literature that is not only becoming vast in scope but increasingly excellent. If the reader wishes to consult a full analytical bibliography, he is advised to see the extensive list appended to Frederick Rudolph's volume, *The American College and University, A History* (New York: Alfred A. Knopf, 1962).

I have thought it may be useful, however, to supply brief lists of two different kinds of books: first, recently published general histories of higher education in this country; and second, works on special aspects of higher education. These lists are by no means exhaustive.

GENERAL HISTORIES OF HIGHER EDUCATION

In this category the number of books that have recently been published is small, and the topic of general histories may be prefaced by mentioning a collection of source materials: *American Higher Education. A Documentary History*, 2 vols., edited by Richard Hofstadter and Wilson Smith (Chicago: University of Chicago Press, 1961). Here the documents have been skillfully chosen and arranged to illustrate the major events in our educational history from the first proposal for a college in the Massachusetts Bay Colony in 1633 to the report of President Truman's Commission on Higher Education for Democracy in 1947. Other recent comprehensive works are the following:

George P. Schmidt's work, *The Liberal Arts College* (New Brunswick: Rutgers University Press, 1957), is a small volume dealing sympathetically and discerningly with the American college from colonial times to the present. Naturally, the greatest attention is paid to the nineteenth century when the college was in its greatest flowering.

John S. Brubacher and Willis Rudy's *Higher Education in Transition; An American History, 1636–1956* (New York: Harper & Brothers, 1958), a single large volume, contains a huge store of information and a good deal of pertinent analysis. The arrangement of the work is erratic, and the volume suffers from congestion. The reader is, however, grateful for the immense scope and the exhaustive bibliography.

In 1952 Richard Hofstadter and C. DeWitt Hardy published an important book, *The Development and Scope of Higher Education in the United States* (New York: Columbia University Press). The first half of the book, written by Hofstadter, is distinguished by its perspective and proportion; it is clear and objective. The second half is less detached in attitude and develops a well-reasoned statement in support of liberal education.

Frederick Rudolph's work, *The American College and University, A History* (New York: Alfred A. Knopf, 1962), is the most satisfactory history of higher education in America yet to appear. It covers the whole subject with form and proportion. It is pithy without sharpness and full without congestion. A large analytical bibliography adds to the value of the book.

The reader desiring a brief account may wish to consult Francis M. Rogers' *Higher Education in the United States: A Summary View* (Cambridge: Harvard University Press, 1960).

STUDIES OF SPECIAL ASPECTS OF EDUCATION

Axt, Richard G., *The Federal Government and Financing Higher Education*. New York: Columbia University Press, 1952.

Aydelotte, Frank, *Honors Courses in American Colleges and Universities*. Washington: Bulletin of the National Research Council, April 1925.

Babbidge, Homer D., Jr., and Robert M. Rosenzweig, *The Federal Interest in Higher Education*. New York: McGraw-Hill Book Company, 1962.

Beck, Hubert P., *The Men Who Control our Universities*. New York: King's Crown Press, 1947.

Berelson, Bernard, *Graduate Education in the United States*. New York: McGraw-Hill Book Company, 1960.

Butts, R. Freeman, *The College Charts Its Course*. New York: McGraw-Hill Book Company, 1939.

Calhoun, David Hovey, *The American Civil Engineer, Origins and Conflict*. Cambridge: Technology Press, 1960.

Caplow, Theodore, and Reece J. McGee, *The Academic Marketplace*. New York: Basic Books, 1958.

Cowling, Donald, and Carter Davidson, *Colleges for Freedom*. New York: Harper and Brothers, 1957.

Curti, Merle, *The Social Ideas of American Educators*. Patterson, N.J.: Littlefield, Adams & Co., rev. ed., 1959.

David, Opal D., *The Education of Women: Signs for the Future*. Washington: American Council on Education, 1959.

Dodds, Harold W., *The Academic President: Educator or Caretaker?* New York: McGraw-Hill Book Co., 1962.

Dupree, A. Hunter, *Science in the Federal Government: A History of Policies and Activities to 1940*. Cambridge: Harvard University Press, 1957.

Dutcher, George Matthew, *An Historical and Critical Survey of the Curriculum of Wesleyan University and Relevant Subjects*. Middletown: Wesleyan University Press, 1948.

Eddy, Edward Danforth, Jr., *Colleges for our Land and Time: The Land-grant Idea in American Education*. New York: Harper and Brothers, 1957.

———— *College Influence on Student Character*. Washington: American Council on Education, 1959.

Foerster, Norman, *The American State University*. Chapel Hill: University of North Carolina Press, 1937.

Fuess, Claude M., *The College Board: Its First Fifty Years*. New York: Columbia University Press, 1950.

Gabriel, Ralph Henry, *Religion and Learning at Yale: The Church of Christ in the College and University, 1757–1957*. New Haven: Yale University Press, 1958.

Habein, Margaret L., *Spotlight on the College Student*. Washington: American Council on Education, 1959.

Hofstadter, Richard, and Walter P. Metzgar, *The Development of Academic Freedom in the United States*. New York: Columbia University Press, 1955.

Hutchins, Robert Maynard, *Higher Learning in America*. New Haven: Yale University Press, 1936.

Jacob, Philip, *Changing Values in College*. New York: Harper and Brothers, 1958.

John, Walton C., *Graduate Study in Universities and Colleges in the United States*. Washington: U.S. Office of Education, Bulletin 20, 1935.

Jones, Howard Mumford, *One Great Society: Humane Learning in the United States*. New York: Harcourt, Brace & Co., 1959.

Knight, Douglas, et al., *The Federal Government and Higher Education*. Englewood Cliffs, N.J.: Prentice-Hall, 1960.

Le Duc, Thomas, *Piety and Intellect at Amherst College, 1865–1912*. New York: Columbia University Press, 1946.

McIver, Robert M., *Academic Freedom in Our Time*. New York: Columbia University Press, 1955.

Mayhew, Lewis B., *General Education: An Account and Appraisal; A Guide for College Faculties*. New York: Harper and Brothers, 1960.

Newcomer, Mabel, *A Century of Higher Education for Women*. New York: Harper and Brothers, 1959.

Orlans, Harold, *The Effects of Federal Programs on Higher Education: A Study of 36 Institutions*. Washington: The Brookings Institution, 1962.

Power, Edward J., *A History of Catholic Education in the United States*. Milwaukee: Bruce Publishing Co., 1958.

Riesman, David, *Constraint and Variety in American Education*. Lincoln: University of Nebraska Press, 1956.

Ross, Earle D., *Democracy's College: The Land-Grant Movement in the Formative Stage*. Ames: Iowa State College Press, 1942.

Ruml, Beardsley, and Sidney G. Tickton, *Teaching Salaries Then and Now: A 50-Year Comparison with Other Occupations and Industries*. New York: Fund for the Advancement of Education, 1955.

Savage, Howard J., et al., *American College Athletics*. New York: Carnegie Foundation for the Advancement of Teaching, 1929.

Smith, Huston, *Purposes of Higher Education*. New York: Harper and Brothers, 1955.

Stoke, Harold W., *The American College President*. New York: Harper and Brothers, 1959.

Storr, Richard J., *The Beginnings of Graduate Education in America*. Chicago: University of Chicago Press, 1958.

Wilson, Logan, *The Academic Man: A Study in the Sociology of a Profession*. New York: Oxford University Press, 1942.

Wriston, Henry M., *Academic Procession*. New York: Columbia University Press, 1959.

Woodburne, Lloyd S., *Faculty Personnel Policies in Higher Education*. New York: Harper and Brothers, 1950.

Woody, Thomas, *A History of Women's Education in the United States*. Lancaster, Pa.: The Science Press, 1929.

NOTES

CHAPTER I. CHARACTERISTICS

1. *Biennial Survey of Education in the United States, 1948–1950* (Washington, Government Printing Office), chapter 4, secs. 1 and 2, pp. 6 and 35. The statistics for 1964 are taken from the projection of student enrollments as tabulated by the Office of Education and reported in *The New York Times* for September 6, 1964, sec. 4, p. E9.

2. *Educational Directory, 1955–56* (Washington, Government Printing Office).

3. *Biennial Survey of Education,* as above in note 1.

4. Clark Kerr, *The Uses of the University* (Cambridge: Harvard University Press, 1963).

5. Turner's epoch-making essay on the forces at work in shaping American society, though influential from the time of its first publication in 1893, was not expanded into the volume, *The Frontier in American History* (New York, Henry Holt & Co.), until 1920. The quotation appears on p. 283.

6. *Universities: American, English, German* (New York: Oxford University Press, 1930), pp. 17–18.

7. Logan Wilson, *The Academic Man* (New York: Oxford University Press, 1942). This illuminating book was published before the much deeper involvement of the academic man during and after the Second World War.

8. William C. DeVane, *The American University in the Twentieth Century, The Davis Washington Mitchell Lectures at Tulane University* (Baton Rouge: Louisiana State University Press, 1957); see pp. 69–72.

CHAPTER II. THE COLLEGE, 1900–1920

1. *The Development of Harvard University Since the Inauguration of President Eliot, 1869–1929,* ed. Samuel Eliot Morison (Cambridge: Harvard University Press, 1930).

2. *Biennial Survey of Education in the United States, 1948–1950,* pp. 6 and 35. By 1950 there were 2,659,021 students in the colleges of the country, and in 1964 there were almost 5 million.

3. Henry Seidel Canby, *Alma Mater: The Gothic Age of the American College* (New York: Farrar and Rinehart, 1936); see especially chaps. 2 and 3, "College Life," and "Education: Common and Preferred." See also

John Brubacher and Willis Rudy, *Higher Education in Transition* (New York: Harper and Brothers, 1958), chap. 7.

4. Canby, pp. 37–38.

5. See Henry Aaron Yeomans, *Abbott Lawrence Lowell, 1856–1943* (Cambridge: Harvard University Press, 1948), p. 338. Hadley and Lowell, according to Yeomans, required their coaches, Camp and Haughton, to introduce this reform in order to reduce the hazards.

6. See Wilbur Cortez Abbott, "The Guild of Students," in *The Atlantic Monthly*, CXXVIII (November 1921), 623ff.

7. "What Is College for?" in *Scribner's Magazine*, XLVI (November 1909), 572–575. For a sharp comment on the colleges, see Thorstein Veblen, *Higher Education in America* (New York: W. B. Huebsch, 1913).

8. See, for example, Charles M. Perry, *Henry Philip Tappan* (Ann Arbor: University of Michigan Press, 1933), p. 232, for the point of view of the famous president of the University of Michigan.

9. Yeomans, chap. 12.

10. This was the opinion of Abraham Flexner expressed in his volume, *The American College* (New York: Century Co., 1908).

11. "President Lowell's Inaugural Address," reprinted in *The Development of Harvard University Since the Inauguration of President Eliot*.

12. *Yale College, An Educational History, 1871–1921* (New Haven: Yale University Press, 1952), chap. 18. This is Vol. I of *Yale: College and University, 1871–1937*.

13. For the several types of teachers Canby found at Yale at the turn of the century, see his vivid analysis in *Alma Mater*, chaps. 4–6. Canby distinguished five schools of the theory of teaching in his time: the hard-boiled, the indifferent, the idealistic, the factual, and the enthusiastic. It is obvious that Canby thought that few professors penetrated the thick shell of undergraduate life, and even fewer had a profound and lasting effect upon their students.

14. *The Development of Harvard University Since the Inauguration of President Eliot*, p. lxxxviv.

CHAPTER III. GRADUATE AND PROFESSIONAL SCHOOLS
BEFORE THE FIRST WORLD WAR

1. See Samuel Eliot Morison, *Three Centuries of Harvard, 1636–1936* (Cambridge: Harvard University Press, 1936); and *The Development of Harvard University Since the Inauguration of President Eliot, 1869–1929*, ed. Samuel Eliot Morison (Cambridge: Harvard University Press, 1930).

2. William James, "The Ph.D. Octopus," in the *Harvard Monthly*, XXXVI, 1–9. The date, 1903, was significant; so was the tone of James's violent attack upon the new academic fashion.

3. George Wilson Pierson, *Yale: College and University, 1871–1937*, 2 vols. (New Haven: Yale University Press, 1952, 1955). See also Ralph Henry Gabriel, *Religion and Learning at Yale: The Church of Christ in the College and University, 1757–1957* (New Haven: Yale University Press, 1958).

4. John C. French, *A History of the University Founded by Johns Hopkins* (Baltimore: Johns Hopkins University Press, 1946); and Hugh Hawkins, *Pioneer: A History of the Johns Hopkins University, 1874–1889* (Ithaca: Cornell University Press, 1960).

5. French, pp. 84, 204–205. For a full account of the General Education movement, see Lewis B. Mayhew, *General Education: An Account and Appraisal; a Guide for College Faculties* (New York: Harper and Brothers, 1960). For a detailed description of Columbia's program, see *A College Program in Action* (New York: Columbia University Press, 1946).

6. Thomas Wakefield Goodspeed, *A History of the University of Chicago Founded by John D. Rockefeller: The First Quarter Century* (Chicago: University of Chicago Press, 1916).

7. Carl Becker, *Cornell University: Founders and the Founding* (Ithaca: Cornell University Press, 1943).

8. Burke A. Hinsdale, *History of the University of Michigan* (Ann Arbor: University of Michigan, 1906); and Kent Sagendorph, *Michigan: The Story of the University* (New York: E. P. Dutton, 1948).

9. James Burrill Angell, *Selected Addresses* (New York: Longmans, Green and Company, 1912), p. 49.

10. Merle Curti and Vernon Carstensen, *The University of Wisconsin: A History, 1848–1925*, 2 vols. (Madison: University of Wisconsin Press, 1949).

11. Richard T. Ely, *The Ground Under Our Feet* (New York: Macmillan Company, 1938), pp. 195–196.

12. Frederick C. Howe, *Wisconsin: An Experiment in Democracy* (New York: Charles Scribner's Sons, 1912), p. 175.

13. *A History of the Faculty of Philosophy, Columbia University*, ed. Jacques Barzun (New York: Columbia University Press, 1957); and Frederick Paul Keppel, *Columbia* (New York: Oxford University Press, 1914).

14. E. E. Slosson, *Great American Universities* (New York: Macmillan Company, 1910), chap. 15. Other interesting statistics concerning the universities in 1908–9 are given in Slosson's book. In total enrollment Chicago, Cornell, Michigan, and Columbia slightly exceeded the figure of 5,000 students, and Johns Hopkins by design was considerably lower at 3,800.

15. *Medical Education in the United States* (New York: Carnegie Foundation for the Advancement of Teaching, Bulletin 4, 1910).

CHAPTER IV. HIGHER EDUCATION BETWEEN TWO WORLD WARS

1. John S. Brubacher and Willis Rudy, *Higher Education in Transition* (New York: Harper and Brothers, 1958), p. 359.

2. Alexander Meiklejohn, *The Experimental College* (New York: Harper and Brothers, 1932).

3. James Gray, *The University of Minnesota, 1851–1951* (Minneapolis: University of Minnesota Press, 1951), pp. 308–322.

4. *An Adventure in Education, Swarthmore College under Frank Aydelotte*, by the Swarthmore College Faculty (New York: Macmillian Company, 1941); and Frank Aydelotte, *Breaking the Academic Lock Step: The Development of Honors Work in American Colleges and Universities* (New York: Macmillan Company, 1944).

5. *A History of Columbia College on Morningside*, ed. Dwight C. Miner (New York: Columbia University Press, 1954).

6. Chauncey Samuel Boucher, *The Chicago College Plan*, Revised and Enlarged after Ten Years' Operation of the Plan by A. J. Brumbaugh (Chicago: University of Chicago Press, 1940).

7. A course in great books had been developed at Columbia by John Erskine as early as 1920. See *A History of Columbia College*, pp. 43–44.

8. *Higher Learning in America* (New Haven: Yale University Press, 1936). This first assault was followed by another volume, *No Friendly Voice* (Chicago: University of Chicago Press, 1936). The title of the later book, drawn from a speech of Satan's in *Paradise Lost*, suggests that Hutchins thought of himself as the devil's advocate.

9. Harry D. Gideonse, *The Higher Learning in a Democracy: A Reply to President Hutchins' Critique of the American University* (New York: Farrar and Rinehart, 1937).

10. See *Biennial Survey of Education in the United States, 1948–1950*, (Washington, Government Printing Office), chap. 4, for these and related statistics.

11. See for these Southern universities the following: Kemp Plumer Battle, *History of the University of North Carolina*, 2 vols. (Raleigh: Edwards and Broughton Printing Co., 1907, 1912); Louis R. Wilson, *The University of North Carolina, 1900–1930: The Making of a Modern University* (Chapel Hill, University of North Carolina Press, 1957); Nora Campbell Chaffin, *Trinity College, 1839–1892: The Beginnings of Duke University* (Durham: Duke University Press, 1950); Edwin Mims, *History of Vanderbilt University* (Nashville: Vanderbilt University Press, 1946); and Henry Morton Bullock, *A History of Emory University* (Nashville: Parthenon Press, 1936).

12. See James Gray, *The University of Minnesota, 1851–1951* (Minneapolis: University of Minnesota Press, 1951); Clarence Ray Aurner,

History of Education in Iowa, 1914–16 (Iowa City: State Historical Society of Iowa, 1914–1920); and Jonas Viles et al., *The University of Missouri: A Centennial History* (Columbia: University of Missouri, 1939). For general accounts, see Richard J. Storr, *The Beginnings of Graduate Education in America* (Chicago: University of Chicago Press, 1953); and Norman Foerster, *The American State Universities* (Chapel Hill: University of North Carolina Press, 1937).

13. See William Warren Ferrier, *Origin and Development of the University of California* (Berkeley: Sather Gate Book Shop, 1930); Enoch Albert Bryan, *Historical Sketch of the State College of Washington, 1890–1925* (Spokane: The Alumni and Associated Students, 1928); and Orrin Leslie Elliott, *Stanford University: The First Twenty-Five Years* (Stanford: Stanford University Press, 1937).

14. Earl James McGrath, *The Evolution of Administrative Offices in Institutions of Higher Education in the United States from 1860 to 1933* (Chicago: private edition, distributed by Chicago University Library, 1938).

15. W. Storrs Lee, *God Bless Our Queer Old Dean* (New York: G. P. Putnam, 1959). For a description of the modern president, see Harold W. Stoke, *The American College President* (New York: Harper and Brothers, 1959); and Harold W. Dodds, *The Academic President: Educator or Caretaker?* (New York, McGraw-Hill Book Co., 1962).

16. See Earl James McGrath, "The Control of Higher Education in America," in *The Educational Record*, XVII (April 1936), 259–272. For a full study of boards of trustees, see Hubert Beck, *Men Who Control Our Universities* (New York: King's Crown Press, 1947).

17. In 1905 Andrew Carnegie set up a fund of $10 million to provide pensions for college teachers. But such was the expansion of the profession and the inflation of the dollar that in a few years the amount proved inadequate. In 1918 the Carnegie Foundation reorganized its pension plan into the Teachers Insurance and Annuity Association.

18. Richard Hofstadter and Walter P. Metzgar, *The Development of Academic Freedom in the United States* (New York: Columbia University Press, 1955).

19. Beardsley Ruml and Sidney G. Tickton, *Teaching Salaries Then and Now* (New York: Fund for the Advancement of Education, Bulletin 1, 1955).

20. Cited by Frederick Rudolph, *The American College and University, A History.* (New York, Alfred A. Knopf, 1962), pp. 196–197.

21. Walton C. John, *Graduate Study in Universities and Colleges in the United States* (Washington: Office of Education, Bulletin 20, 1935). See also Bernard Berelson, *Graduate Education in the United States* (New York: McGraw-Hill Book Co., 1960).

CHAPTER V. UNIVERSITY STUDIES

1. In the comments on science in this chapter I am indebted to a number of books, but especially to *Education in the Age of Science*, ed. Brand Blanshard (New York: Basic Books, 1959), and to three reports of the President's Science Advisory Committee: "Strengthening American Science," December 27, 1958; "Education for the Age of Science," May 24, 1959; and "Scientific Progress, the Universities, and the Federal Government," November 15, 1960 (Washington, Government Printing Office).

2. See *Education in the Age of Science*, p. 203. The passage is by Ernest Nagel in sec. 4, "Science and the Humanities."

3. Part of the material in this section is drawn from the report of the Behavioral Sciences Subpanel, "Strengthening the Behavioral Sciences." *Science V*, April 20, 1962 (Washington, Government Printing Office).

4. See John Maynard Keynes, *The Economic Consequences of the Peace* (New York: Harcourt, Brace and Howe, 1920); *A Treatise on Probability* (London: Macmillan Company, 1921); *A Tract on Monetary Reform* (New York: Harcourt, Brace and Howe, 1923); and *The End of Laissez-Faire* (London: Hogarth Press, 1926). The volume that had such an enormous effect upon economic thinking, however, is *The General Theory of Employment, Interest and Money* (London: Macmillan Company, 1936), significantly a product of the depression.

5. Robert S. and Helen Merrell Lynd, *Middletown: A Study in Contemporary American Culture* (New York: Harcourt, Brace and Co, 1929).

6. *The Lonely Crowd: A Study of the Changing American Character*, in collaboration with Ruel Denney and Nathan Glazer (1950), and *Faces in the Crowd* (1952) have been influential in social thought in recent years. The fact that Riesman received his scholarly training at the University of Chicago is significant. Both books were published in New Haven by Yale University Press.

7. See, for example, Carleton S. Coon, *The Races of Europe* (New York: Macmillan Company, 1939).

8. *American Historical Review* XXXVII, 233–234. This essay later appeared in Becker's book, *Everyman His Own Historian* (New York: F. S. Crofts & Co., 1935).

9. Turner's essay was expanded into a book, *The Frontier in American History* (New York: Henry Holt & Co., 1920).

10. See the bibliography at the end of this volume. Schmidt's work, though excellent, is limited in scope; Brubacher and Rudy's is full of information and is comprehensive, but is arranged poorly; Rudolph's is the most satisfactory historical account of higher education in America that has yet appeared.

11. The classics maintained its association and periodicals, such as *Classical Philology,* and continued to attract a number of very able scholars; but the more rapidly growing association was that of scholars in modern European languages, the Modern Language Association, founded in 1883, with its journal, *PMLA.*

12. In the account that follows I am indebted primarily to two publications: René Wellek's chapter on "Literary Scholarship" in *American Scholarship in the Twentieth Century,* ed. Merle Curti (Cambridge: Harvard University Press, 1953); and Douglas Bush's essay, "Literary Scholarship and Criticism," in *Liberal Education,* XLVII (May 1961), 207–228.

13. Albert Stanburrough Cook of Yale was a typical scholar of the time in the philological tradition. See his admirable expression of the ideal in *The Higher Study of English* (Boston: Houghton Mifflin and Company, 1906). Unfortunately, the practice of Cook and most of the adherents of the ideal fell short in the results.

14. A few samples of early excellent work in this kind of scholarship may be cited here: C. F. Tucker Brooke, *The Shakespeare Apocrypha* (Oxford: Clarendon Press, 1908), and *The Works of Christopher Marlowe* (Oxford: Clarendon Press, 1910); G. L. Kittredge, *A Study of Gawain and the Green Knight* (Cambridge: Harvard University Press, 1916); Thomas W. Baldwin, *Organization and Personnel of the Shakespearean Company* (Princeton: Princeton University Press, 1927); James D. Bruce, *The Evolution of the Arthurian Romance,* 2 vols. (Baltimore: Johns Hopkins University Press, 1923); Roger S. Loomis, *Celtic Myth and Arthurian Romance* (New York: Columbia University Press, 1927); Raymond D. Havens, *The Influence of Milton in English Poetry* (Cambridge: Harvard University Press, 1922); and George McLean Harper, *William Wordsworth: His Life, Works and Influence* (New York: Charles Scribner's Sons, 1916).

15. See C. B. Tinker, *Nature's Simple Plan* (Princeton: Princeton University Press, 1922); Hoxie Fairchild, *The Noble Savage* (New York: Columbia University Press, 1928); and Lois Whitney, *Primitivism and the Idea of Progress* (Baltimore: Johns Hopkins University Press, 1934).

16. As characteristic examples of their work, see Cleanth Brooks, *Modern Poetry and the Tradition* (Chapel Hill: University of North Carolina Press, 1939), and *The Well Wrought Urn* (New York: Reynal and Hitchcock, 1947); F. O. Matthiessen, *The Achievement of T. S. Eliot* (New York and Oxford: Oxford University Press, 1935, 2nd ed., 1947), and *The American Renaissance* (New York: Oxford University Press, 1941).

17. *Sewanee Review,* LI (1943), 59.

18. Douglas Bush, "Literary Scholarship and Criticism", in *Liberal Education,* XLVII (May 1961), 217.

19. The most significant works in this field are René Wellek's compre-

hensive *History of Criticism,* 3 vols. (New Haven: Yale University Press, 1955, 1955, 1962; 4th vol. not yet published); William Wimsatt and Cleanth Brooks, *Literary Criticism: A Short History* (New York: Alfred A. Knopf, 1957); Harry Levin, *Contexts of Criticism* (Cambridge: Harvard University Press, 1957); and René Wellek and Austin Warren, *Theory of Literature* (New York: Harcourt, Brace and Co., 1949). One should also note Herbert Muller, *Science and Criticism* (New Haven: Yale University Press, 1943).

20. See, as examples, William Wimsatt, *Prose Style of Samuel Johnson,* (New Haven: Yale University Press, 1941); and Walter J. Bate, *From Classic to Romantic: Premises of Taste in Eighteenth-Century England* (Cambridge: Harvard University Press, 1946).

21. See the admirable chapter, "Philosophical Scholarship," by Arthur E. Murphy in *American Scholarship in the Twentieth Century,* ed. Curti. See also Brand Blanshard's analyses of logical positivism and existentialism in "The Changing Climate of Philosophy," in *Liberal Education,* XLVII (May 1961), 229–254.

22. Royce's most effective works are *The World and the Individual,* 2 vols., 1889, 1901; *The Philosophy of Loyalty,* 1908; and *The Hope of the Great Community,* 1916. All were published by Macmillan Company, New York.

23. See Philip Wiener, *Evolution and the Founders of Pragmatism* (Cambridge: Harvard University Press, 1949). Peirce's work appears in *Collected Papers of Charles Sanders Peirce,* 6 vols., ed. Charles Hartshorne and Paul Weiss (Cambridge: Harvard University Press, 1931–1935; reissued in 3 vols., 1960).

24. *The American Mind* (New Haven: Yale University Press, 1950), p. 97. Among Dewey's many books the following are most pertinent here: *Studies in Logical Theory* (Chicago: University of Chicago Press, 1903); *The Influence of Darwin on Philosophy* (New York: Henry Holt and Co., 1910); *Liberalism and Social Action* (New York: G. P. Putnam's Sons, 1935); and *Logic* (New York: Henry Holt and Co., 1938). See also his *Education and Democracy* (New York: Macmillan Company, 1916).

25. Books carrying weight at the time were Sidney Hook, *Towards the Understanding of Karl Marx* (New York: John Day, 1933); Harold Laski, *The State in Theory and Practice* (New York: Viking Press, 1935); and Beatrice and Sidney Webb, *Soviet Communism: A New Civilization,* 2 vols. (New York: Charles Scribner's Sons, 1936).

26. Gilson's influential books for this movement were *The Spirit of Medieval Philosophy* (New York: Charles Scribner's Sons, 1936), and *The Unity of Philosophical Experience* (New York: Charles Scribner's Sons, 1937). So also was George Santayana's *Realms of Being* (New York: Charles Scribner's Sons, 1940).

27. Lovejoy's *Revolt Against Dualism* (New York: W. W. Norton, 1930) was a brilliant contribution in this field, and Cohen, in *Reason and Nature* (New York: Harcourt, Brace and Co., 1931), showed how effective the methods of this school could be in legal and political problems.

28. The movement was clarified by Clarence I. Lewis, *Mind and the World Order* (New York: Charles Scribner's Sons, 1929).

29. Kierkegaard's volumes have been excellently translated as *Philosophical Fragments* (Princeton: Princeton University Press, 1936), and *Concluding Unscientific Postscript* (Princeton: Princeton University Press, 1941).

30. Blanshard's pertinent work is entitled *The Nature of Thought*, 2 vols. (New York: Macmillan Company, 1940); Lewis' is *An Analysis of Knowledge and Valuation* (LaSalle, Ill.: Open Court, 1946); Murphy's is *The Uses of Reason* (New York: Macmillan Company, 1943); and Black's is *Philosophical Analysis* (Ithaca: Cornell University Press, 1950).

31. Henry Adams' essay, "The Rule of Phase Applied to History," was written in 1909, but first published in Brooks Adams' edition of *Degradation of the Democratic Dogma* (New York: Macmillan Company, 1919). See also *The Education of Henry Adams* (Boston: Houghton Mifflin Company, 1930), chap. 25, "The Dynamo and the Virgin."

CHAPTER VI. THE FEDERAL GOVERNMENT AND HIGHER EDUCATION

1. In this chapter I am especially indebted to the following books: Charles V. Kidd, *American Universities and Federal Research* (Cambridge: Harvard University Press, 1959); *The Federal Government and Higher Education*, ed. Douglas Knight for the American Assembly (Englewood Cliffs: Prentice-Hall, 1960); Homer D. Babbidge and Robert M. Rosenzweig, *The Federal Interest in Higher Education* (New York: McGraw-Hill Book Co., 1962); Charles A. Quattlebaum, *Federal Educational Policies, Programs and Proposals* (Washington: Government Printing Office, 1960); and the pamphlet, *A Survey of Federal Programs in Higher Education*, by J. Kenneth Little, prepared for the Office of Education, Department of Health, Education and Welfare (Washington: Government Printing Office, 1962). The selected bibliography of this last document is most useful for its references to recent volumes and articles on the many phases of the relation between the government and higher education.

2. See, for example, the account of the struggle between Yale College and the Connecticut Assembly in Edmund S. Morgan's *The Gentle Puritan: A Life of Ezra Stiles, 1727–1795* (New Haven: Yale University Press, 1962), chap. 25, "The Great Reconciliation."

3. See the government publication, *Land-Grant Colleges and Univer-*

sities: A Federal-State Partnership (Washington: Office of Education, Bulletin 21, 1952). See also Edward Danforth Eddy, Jr., *Colleges for Our Land and Time: The Landgrant Idea in American Education* (New York: Harper and Brothers, 1957).

4. See *Science, The Endless Frontier* (Washington: National Science Foundation, 1945). See especially the reprint of this volume, dated 1960, with Alan T. Waterman's valuable introduction. The modesty of Bush's plan for the government's involvement in science, as well as his imaginative insight, is clearly to be seen here (pp. xxiv, xxv). See also *Science and Public Policy* (Washington: Government Printing Office, 1947), the report of the President's Scientific Research Board. It is these documents that moved science and engineering to the center of the government's operations in defense of the country through research, development, and the training of personnel. The development of major programs in health followed somewhat later.

5. Quoted in Babbidge and Rosenzweig, p. 25.

6. See the National Science Foundation's *Review of Data on Research and Development,* April 1960. See also Kidd, *passim.*

7. The table is taken from *A Survey of Federal Programs in Higher Education,* p. 6. The percentages do not include funds for the operation of government-owned research centers.

8. Kidd, p. 5. For a summary of the "Current Policies and Programs" of each of the sponsoring government agencies, see *The Federal Government and Higher Education,* pp. 63–71.

9. These figures are taken from Babbidge and Rosenzweig, p. 53. Congress later had some regrets in allowing such a range of studies to qualify.

10. See the amusing imaginary dialogue between the representative of the government and the university research administrator in the section called "Federal Sponsorship of University Research," in *The Federal Government and Higher Education,* pp. 107–121.

11. See *A Survey of Federal Programs in Higher Education,* pp. 4–9.

12. *Ibid.,* p. 2.

13. Quoted by Babbidge and Rosenzweig, p. 145. A more generous statement of the position of the Land Grant organization may be seen on p. 112.

14. The most useful and significant book upon this matter is Harold Orlans, *The Effects of Federal Programs on Higher Education: A Study of 36 Institutions,* prepared for the Brookings Institution (Washington, 1962). Orlans, though generally most fair, is inclined to see the matter from the point of view of Washington.

15. On August 17, 1964, Congressman William S. Moorhead introduced a bill (HR 12406) to establish a National Humanities Foundation com-

parable to the National Science Foundation, but no action has yet been taken.

16. Richard G. Axt, *The Federal Government and Financing Higher Education* (New York: Columbia University Press, 1952); see pp. 14–15.

17. Babbidge and Rosenzweig, p. 153.

CHAPTER VII. AMERICAN HIGHER EDUCATION TODAY

1. Divisional honors majors are provided at Yale under the categories history, the arts and letters; politics and economics; and culture and behavior. As in many other institutions, interdisciplinary majors are also offered in several area studies.

2. Harold Taylor was the chief spokesman for the progressive college. See Harold Taylor et al., *Essays in Teaching* (New York: Harper and Brothers, 1950); also, Algo D. Henderson and Dorothy Hall, *Antioch College: Its Design for General Education* (New York: Harper and Brothers, 1946).

3. See *General Education: An Account and Appraisal; a Guide for College Faculties,* ed. Lewis B. Mayhew (New York: Harper and Brothers, 1960); *A History of Columbia College on Morningside,* ed. Dwight C. Miner (New York: Columbia University Press, 1954), pp. 46–47; and *The Idea and Practice of General Education,* by the University of Chicago Faculty (Chicago: University of Chicago Press, 1950).

4. Jacques Barzun, "College to University—and After," an address delivered on December 11, 1963, at the convocation celebrating the first year of Hofstra's existence as a university. I had arrived at the same general conclusion in a paper entitled "The College of Liberal Arts," written in the summer of 1963 for publication in the Autumn 1964 issue of *Daedalus.* See also my article, "A Time and Place for Liberal Education," in *Reflections on the Role of Liberal Education,* a special issue of the periodical *Liberal Education* (May 1964).

5. For the amounts loaned under Title II of the NDEA and other pertinent data, see tables 13 and 14 on pp. 125–126 in the American Council on Education's study, *Twenty-Six Campuses and the Federal Government* (Washington, 1963). This document is reprinted as a part of the *Fifty-Eighth Annual Report of the Carnegie Foundation for the Advancement of Teaching, 1962–63;* the tables in the Carnegie Report are on pp. 53–54.

6. See "The Graduate School Today and Tomorrow," produced by the Committee of Fifteen for the Fund for the Advancement of Education of the Ford Foundation in 1955. The recommendations of the committee were conventional. See also Bernard Berelson, *Graduate Education in the United States* (New York: McGraw-Hill Book Co., 1960).

7. "Twenty-Six Campuses and the Federal Government," in *The Educational Record*, XLIV (April 1963), 97; reprinted in the Carnegie Report, p. 12. Most of the figures used here are taken from this document.

8. See David Boroff, "That Science Center Called MIT," *The New York Times Magazine*, August 18, 1963.

9. National Science Foundation, *Federal Funds for Science* (Washington: Government Printing Office, 1961), appendix B.

10. "Twenty-Six Campuses," *The Educational Record*, p. 119; reprinted in the Carnegie Report, p. 46.

11. See the *Annual Report*, 1963, by Caryl Parker Haskins, president of the Carnegie Institution of Washington; and Harold Orlans, *The Effects of Federal Programs on Higher Education, a Study of 36 Institutions* (Washington: Brookings Institution, 1962).

12. See *The Educational Record*, pp. 106–115; reprinted in the Carnegie Report, pp. 23–40. See also Theodore Caplow and Reece J. McGee, *The Academic Marketplace* (New York: Basic Books, 1958).

13. Abraham Flexner, *Medical Education in the United States*, Carnegie Foundation for the Advancement of Teaching, Bulletin 4 (New York, 1910).

EPILOGUE. THE DILEMMA OF NATIONAL GREATNESS

1. See Charles Percy Snow, *The Two Cultures and the Scientific Revolution*, The Rede Lecture (Cambridge, Eng.: Cambridge University Press, 1959); and *Science and Government*, The Godkin Lectures (Cambridge: Harvard University Press, 1961). For Snow's reply to his critics, see "The Two Cultures: A Second Look," in *The Times Literary Supplement*, October 25, 1963, pp. 839–844.

2. John Tyndall, *Address Delivered Before the British Association Assembled at Belfast* (New York: D. Appleton and Company, rev. ed., 1875), p. 94.

3. Arnold's lecture, "Literature and Science," given at Cambridge University in 1882, was also a Rede Lecture, the same foundation upon which Snow later lectured. Arnold's essay was published in a volume, *Discourses in America*, in 1885.

4. Correlli Barnett, *The Swordbearers* (London: Eyre and Spottiswoode, 1963).

5. *Ibid.*, p. 183.

6. *Idem.*

7. *Measure for Measure*, II, ii, 107–109.

INDEX